STICKY
BRANDING

STICKY
BRANDING

12.5 Principles to Stand Out,
Attract Customers &
Grow an Incredible Brand

JEREMY MILLER

DUNDURN
TORONTO

Editor: Michael Melgaard
Design: Laura Boyle
Cover Design: Paul Sveda, DesignandDevelop.com
Image Credits: Paul Sveda, DesignandDevelop.com
Printer: Webcom

Library and Archives Canada Cataloguing in Publication

Miller, Jeremy, 1977-, author
    Sticky branding : 12.5 principles to stand out, attract customers,
and grow an incredible brand / Jeremy Miller.

Includes bibliographical references and index.
Issued in print and electronic formats.

ISBN 978-1-4597-2810-3 (pbk.).—ISBN 978-1-4597-2811-0 (pdf).-- ISBN 978-1-4597-2812-7 (epub)

1. Branding (Marketing). I. Title.

HF5415.1255.M54 2015   658.8'27   C2014-906770-4
                                                C2014-906771-2

5   19   18   17   16

  Canada

ONTARIO ARTS COUNCIL
CONSEIL DES ARTS DE L'ONTARIO
an Ontario government agency
un organisme du gouvernement de l'Ontario

We acknowledge the support of the **Canada Council for the Arts** and the **Ontario Arts Council** for our publishing program. We also acknowledge the financial support of the **Government of Canada** through the **Canada Book Fund** and **Livres Canada Books**, and the **Government of Ontario** through the **Ontario Book Publishing Tax Credit** and the **Ontario Media Development Corporation**.

Care has been taken to trace the ownership of copyright material used in this book. The author and the publisher welcome any information enabling them to rectify any references or credits in subsequent editions.

J. Kirk Howard, President

The publisher is not responsible for websites or their content unless they are owned by the publisher.

Printed and bound in Canada.

VISIT US AT
Dundurn.com | @dundurnpress | Facebook.com/dundurnpress | Pinterest.com/dundurnpress

DUNDURN
3 Church Street, Suite 500
Toronto, Ontario, Canada
M5E 1M2

MIX
Paper from
responsible sources
FSC® C004071

Table of Contents

Preface

A winning strategy today may not prevail tomorrow. It might not even be relevant tomorrow.

— *David Aaker, professor emeritus at the Haas School of Business*

Do your customers choose you first?

In 2004 I asked myself that question every day. I'd left a cushy job selling software systems to big companies in order to join my family's IT staffing business. I thought I had what it took to drive sales, and I planned to take the company to the next level. I quickly learned I was mistaken. The wheels were falling off the bus and I didn't know what to do.

During the nineties the sales team at my family's company could generate new clients and business opportunities every week. Through diligent prospecting and by building solid client relationships, the company had become successful. But by the time I joined in 2004, the market had changed and sales had slowed to a crawl.

The sales force had been reeling in a challenging marketplace for over three years. The economy was working against them. Clients had reduced their orders because many had exhausted their IT budgets preparing their computer systems for Y2K. Several software and technology clients had simply disappeared as part of the fallout from the dotcom bubble bursting. A short recession following the tragic events on September 11, 2001, compounded all of these issues.

The impact of these forces had a direct effect on the company's sales performance. What used to take our sales reps a week to achieve was now taking them a month.

I had been groomed on sales training programs like Huthwaite's *Spin Selling* and Miller Heiman's *Strategic Selling*, with a little Tom Hopkins for good measure. Those programs teach you how to find decision makers, build value propositions, and negotiate and win sales deals. I turned to them first when my business faced a sales problem. My logic was that if sales were flagging, then we had to get better at selling. We pushed and pushed, trying to improve our sales process for the better part of a year, but it didn't work.

Our sales guys were doing all they could to find new business opportunities, but more and more we relied on cold calling, advertising, and direct marketing tactics just to keep the sales funnel full. And I have to say, it was a grind. I was the director of business development, but I found myself in the trenches dialing for dollars just to keep the business going. And I hate cold calling! But what else could I do? When the business isn't there, you dig down and you work harder — especially if it's your family's business.

But working harder didn't improve our situation. It actually got worse. Not only were we expending four times the amount of effort to bring in the same amount of business, we were bringing in the wrong clients. My parents had built their business based on strong relationships and partnerships with their clients, but we had to scrape the bottom of the barrel in 2004. We had to take on clients that did not value our services. We were desperate. We took on clients that were unprofitable, unethical, and unpleasant to work with. The revenue wasn't there. The client demand wasn't there. We were firing on all cylinders, but not gaining any traction. We had to change.

To turn around the company we analyzed our business, our market, and what we thought it would take to succeed in our industry. Our findings shocked us. It wasn't our salespeople or our sales processes that was failing us, it was our brand. That realization led to a major rebranding of our business, and it was the catalyst that brought me into a decade-long study of how small- and medium-sized companies innovate and grow recognizable and memorable brands — what I call "Sticky Brands."

As a company, we became highly aware of our brand and our place in the market. I studied our business, customers, and market, and I discovered that our business was indistinguishable from the competition. All of the companies in our industry looked the same. We offered the same services with similar features and benefits. Even our brochures and websites looked alike. Our value propositions — the sum of the benefits a company offers its customers for their products and services — were virtually identical.

We claimed our firm was unique, but from the customers' point of view we looked the same as every other recruiting firm. We were just another tree in the evergreen forest. The large national firms were winning, but only because they stood out as the oldest and most credible trees in the forest. It was no wonder customers weren't choosing us first. If we wanted to win, we couldn't be like everyone else. We had to give customers a compelling reason to choose us. We had to stand out in our industry.

The changes to our brand came fast and furious: a new name, new positioning, and a new approach.

We changed the company name from Miller & Associates, a name that meant nothing to customers who hadn't worked with us before, to the more memorable LEAPJob. Our new brand identity played on the phrase "leap frog." It was bright, energetic, and youthful. We stopped looking like a professional services firm and created a destination for sales and marketing professionals to advance their careers.

Next, we changed the firm's positioning. Previously our focus had been on IT staffing — we recruited software developers, business analysts, project managers, quality assurance specialists, IT managers, and a variety of other technical positions for large companies. It is a well-defined niche in the recruiting industry, and we had been focused on the space for fifteen years. But when we looked at our struggling company and really considered our strengths and passions, it became obvious we had to choose a new niche for our services.

Our real strength was in working with sales and marketing professionals. That is what we geeked out on — it was our passion. But until we were forced to re-evaluate our company we had never really considered delivering this passion and expertise in sales and marketing to our clients. Rather, we focused it internally and used it to develop our own business. We saw ourselves as IT recruiters, not experts in branding, sales, and marketing.

Once we acknowledged our expertise and passion, we knew where the firm could thrive. We repositioned the company to specialize in sales and marketing recruitment. The niche was under-served, and we could become the de facto leader of the space. And that's what we did. LEAPJob became the most recognized sales and marketing recruiting agency in the Greater Toronto Area.

Finally, we changed our approach. This was the most important part of our brand transition. We didn't put lipstick on the proverbial pig. We changed our services, implemented new software systems, delivered a lot of staff training, and rethought how we ran our business. We invested in technology and created a website that sold as well as our best salesperson. And we invested a great deal of time and resources to understand search engine optimization, social media, and content marketing so that we could reach and engage customers in entirely new ways.

We didn't go through evolutionary change, we went through revolutionary change. It was a painful and scary transition. We were charting a lot of unknown waters and making decisions with not much data. Not all our ideas paid off, but the big ones did. Within nine months of rebranding the business, LEAPJob turned the corner and moved back into profitability and growth.

From 2005 to when we sold the company in 2013, LEAPJob did not make a single cold call. The phone rang weekly with new clients and new opportunities. The brand generated at least a client a week, and in peak periods it generated a client a day. The pace didn't even let up during the great recession of 2009 and 2010. The phone kept ringing and our sales were consistent.

This experience was a wake-up call. I learned that you can choose to be just another supplier in your industry, or you can choose to stand out like an orange tree in an evergreen forest. I learned that when your company innovates and stands out, it functions as a beacon that attracts new customers and brings previous customers back. And I learned that it's rewarding to take pride in your brand. Growing a Sticky Brand not only gave me purpose, it gave the whole team a reason to come to work and give it their all. We were all motivated by what we were achieving, and how our actions increased revenue, profit, and growth.

This is your opportunity too. Turning around my family's business was the catalyst for this book. As I went through the experience, I wished I had a book to help guide me and point me in the right direction. Over the past decade I have built on the lessons I learned while rebranding my business. I have researched, profiled, and worked with small- and mid-sized companies from around the world to understand how they are growing incredible brands. This book distills my experiences, and provides you 12.5 Principles to grow your company into a Sticky Brand.

Introduction

You can spot businesses with Sticky Brands in almost every industry. Companies like Apple, Nike, and Starbucks have invested to grow captivating brands, and they are as successful as they are recognizable. But large companies aren't the only ones who can stand out. Any business of any size can turn itself into a Sticky Brand. It's achievable for anyone willing to put in the time, energy, resources, and creativity to break away from the industry norms and find innovative ways to serve their customers.

This is a book about branding written for small- and medium-sized companies that have a marketing budget, but not a vast one. Even if you do not have a lot of resources, these principles can be applied to grow your brand. This is not a book on how Apple or Starbucks grow global brands and why you should emulate them. This is your book on how to grow your brand, and how to make it sticky.

Small- and medium-sized companies are the lifeblood of the North American economy. According to the U.S. Census Bureau there are over 1,260,000 companies in the United States that employ between ten to one thousand employees, and they exist across all sectors: manufacturing, distribution, professional services, construction, retail, food and beverage, information technology — the list continues.[1] Small businesses, companies with fewer than ten employees, are even more plentiful.

Many of these organizations are privately-held and owned and operated by individuals, partners, or families. These are people who take great pride in their companies, their staff, their products, and their brands.

The challenge for small- and mid-sized companies is that there are not many places to turn for relevant marketing and branding ideas. I faced this challenge when I rebranded my family's business. I was a sales guy who had lost his competitive advantage and I wanted to master the skills of branding. I went out of my way to read every branding, marketing, and business book I could get my hands on. I devoured them all. This was all new territory for me, and I wanted to learn from the experts.

What I found was the standard marketing and branding books are geared toward big companies. I was forced to ask, "How is this information relevant for me?" The way Apple and General Electric approach their marketing is radically different from a mid-market company. Global brands have fundamentally different marketing and branding strategies than small- and mid-sized companies. The differences are obvious when you consider the marketing budgets, resources, and influence each size of company has at its disposal.

Apple spent over $1 billion on advertising in 2012,[2] and that's only a piece of its overall marketing reach. Apple's brand radiates through its products' function and design, the app ecosystem, the retail channel, events, and other marketing initiatives. It has a marketing budget that most companies just can't comprehend. There's no point trying to emulate Apple's marketing strategies and tactics; its needs are completely different from yours and mine.

Even if the approach and needs are different, that doesn't mean that growing a Sticky Brand is any less relevant for small- and mid-sized companies. These companies are under immense pressure to innovate and remain competitive. The sales and marketing strategies that worked a decade ago, five years ago, or even a year ago are losing relevance. The mid-market needs a new playbook to stand out and thrive in this very challenging and competitive marketplace. Good salespeople and an attractive website are not enough.

The World Has Changed

Advancements in technology, telecommunications, and globalization are all coming together to reshape how companies compete and how customers buy. I like to compare these shifts with an analogy: "You could walk from Chicago to New York, but why?" Technology gives you far faster and easier ways to get there.

In 1900 the average travel speed in the United States was eight miles an hour. That's a little faster than walking. Fast-forward fifty years, and the velocity of travel accelerated to twenty-five miles an hour. Fast-forward again to 2000, and the rate of travel increased to seventy miles an hour.[3] In the span of a century technology accelerated our rate of movement by close to nine times. That's astonishing.

Companies are facing a similar situation. The strategies and tactics that worked a decade ago are losing relevance. They are like walking. Yes, you can still apply those tactics, but why? The world has changed.

From a business context you are not limited to manufacturing, marketing, or selling in your backyard. The advancements in transportation allow us to move from one point to another with very little resistance. They compress our world and increase our reach. We can market, sell, and service clients in almost any country. Geography is not a limiting factor.

The reverse is true too. You're not simply competing with the firms in your area, you are competing with everyone. For the longest time, a company could sustain a competitive advantage based on its location. Its local infrastructure, branch offices, and proximity to clients created a competitive advantage, but advancements in transportation and communications have eroded those advantages.

Modern smartphones are incredible devices, and in many cases they are more powerful than the PCs we used in 2000. The advancements of telecommunications, the Internet, and social media over the past decade are equivalent to the acceleration of transportation between 1900 to 2000. We have moved from walking to flight in less than a decade. The ramifications of that on how you grow your business and your brand are profound.

These shifts have increased the complexity of your business. Your customers have so many more ways to interact with your brand. There are traditional routes, such as face-to-face, phone, email, and your website. On top of that there are search engines, social media sites, the media, review sites, apps, and more. The digital world and the brick-and-mortar world have merged into one.

Customers don't distinguish the quality of your business based on one channel alone. They expect a consistent experience no matter where they find you. A great face-to-face sales call can be undone by an out-of-date website. The divergent experiences create dissonance in the individual's mind. The positive memories of the face-to-face meeting start to erode as doubts and uncertainty are drawn in from the negative online experience. Worse still if they take a few extra seconds to Google the competition, you can lose them entirely.

Your brand encompasses every customer touch point, in-person or digital. How you manage and control that experience directly influences your bottom line. The stickier your brand, the easier it is to attract and retain clients. And the more clients you attract and retain, the more profitable your business can become.

Managing your brand isn't a choice. The world has changed. Branding has shifted from a specialized, feel-good marketing activity to an essential component of your business. A small or mid-sized company's brand strategy and positioning used to be fairly static. It could operate for seven, ten, or even twenty years without many major revisions to its sales and marketing approach. A company did not have websites, social media, and global competition forcing it to perform at such high standards.

Now, all companies have to take their brand seriously. The choice is whether your brand will be sticky or not. Are you going to push harder for your customers and innovate? Are you going to create a brand experience that is captivating and converts customers into fans? Are you going to challenge the status quo and carve your own path?

If you make these choices, this book will provide you with a playbook to manage and grow your company into a Sticky Brand.

Sticky Branding Defined

Growing a Sticky Brand is a choice. It's a choice to stand out and be remarkable. It's a choice to build meaningful relationships with your customers. It's a choice to cut your own path and innovate in your industry. It's a choice to stand out, attract customers, and drive sales.

But what is a Sticky Brand?

Sticky Brands have something captivating and special about them — they draw customers to them. And once the customer buys, they realize the outside was only a piece of what makes the business special.

You can experience this dynamic by imagining a hot new restaurant opening in your neighborhood. Before your first visit you hear the buzz. Your friends and colleagues rave about their experience and suggest you try it too. You might see the reviews and write-ups in your local newspaper, and you can see the comments online. But until you try the restaurant for yourself, you are only experiencing the external qualities of the brand.

The magic happens when you visit the restaurant and the experience not only lives up to the hype, it exceeds it. The ambiance is great and the food is even better. The more you visit the restaurant, the more you get to know the people and form a bond and a relationship with the business. Each experience builds on the last, and soon the restaurant becomes your first choice when dining out. The restaurant has built a Sticky Brand.

Sticky Brands bring together purpose, vision, customer service, passion, operational excellence, and strategy to deliver remarkable customer experiences. Customers don't beat a path to the company's door because of its marketing. Marketing hype scratches off quickly. Customers seek out Sticky Brands — and come back again and again — because those companies offer a compelling service and a memorable experience.

There are two points of view to a Sticky Brand: an internal perspective and an external one. The internal perspective is how you talk about your brand inside your company. When you talk about your company's brand internally you are often discussing your vision, values, and an ideal of what you are striving to deliver to your customers. The external perspective of your brand is what your customers, suppliers, and the market perceives. This is shaped by the work your company has done and the impression it has left on the market. The external perspective of your brand is the experience your company has delivered.

When both perspectives work together, a corporate brand is strong. The internal team delivers the products, services, and experiences they strive for, and customers are having the desired experience and getting what they expect. The perspectives are in harmony, and the company is fulfilling its purpose and goals.

A Sticky Brand challenges the status quo of its industry and continually asks, "How can we serve our customers better?" That question inevitably leads the company to innovate at all levels of the business: products and services, customer service, design, corporate culture, new sales channels or go-to-market strategies, or some other aspect of its business.

The net result of these innovations is better performance. The company makes deliberate choices to improve its services and customer experience, and that differentiates it from competitors. These innovations allow the brand to stand out, attract customers, and drive sales.

Win the Ties, Repeat the Buys

Sticky Brands deliver results. When your brand stands out it helps differentiate your company from the competitors and win the ties. And when you deliver a remarkable experience, your customers come back again and again and repeat the buys.

Let's explore this idea further.

Win the Ties

Customers have choice, lots of choice. When customers cannot distinguish one option from the next, they tend to default to one of three choices. They will go with what they already know, what's cheapest, or what's available.

Relationships, price, and availability are not effective ways to differentiate your business from the herd. Sticky Brands rise above the crowd and win the ties, because they approach their industry from a unique perspective. They don't look like everyone else. They have an energy and a buzz about them that makes them appear far more compelling. They win the ties, because they stand out.

Repeat the Buys

A brand isn't sticky without repeat customers. Winning a customer once is great, but if your customers are not coming back again and again, there is something wrong. Sticky Brands have substance and deliver clear customer results. Customers come back repeatedly, because they appreciate the service, they like the products, and they are getting the results they want and expect. Repeating the buys is an ideal position, because it is far more efficient and effective to serve a loyal customer than to constantly be hunting for your next one.

Sticky Brands win the ties and repeat the buys. They create a brand experience that is so compelling that they are able to convert their customers into fans. That makes everything easier for the business. Selling becomes easier. Service becomes easier. And that frees up resources to do even better work for their clients.

Growing a Sticky Brand is an ideal worth chasing. Your company will do better work, attract and retain better employees, work with better customers, and be more profitable. Growing a Sticky Brand will grow a stronger business.

Ideas Steeped in Experience

You gain insight from your peers that you cannot gain anywhere else. This book is built on that belief.

A few years ago I sat down with Rob Bracey, the CEO of Quartet Service. I was on my toes the first time I met him because Rob is outgoing, gregarious, and wickedly smart. He's the ultimate CEO, and he has done an impressive job growing Quartet.

Quartet is an IT services company that provides outsourced IT, cloud services, telephony, and IT consulting for mid-market companies. Rob bought the company three days after it went into receivership in 2002. The company was hit hard with the economic downturn following 9/11, and was losing relevancy. Within ten years of the purchase, Rob and his team increased the company's revenue from $2.5 million to over $12 million. Now with sixty-five employees, it continues to grow steadily each year.

Within the first five minutes of meeting Rob he said, "I don't listen to consultants like I do with other CEOs. When I hear the CEO of another firm speak, I listen. I try to figure out where they're coming from, and try to walk a mile in their shoes." He continued, "I don't hear consultants the same way. They say some really smart stuff, but it doesn't resonate as well. They are not my peers."

Rob's comments hit me like a ton of bricks. He is absolutely right. We learn from our peers because they are speaking the same language and sharing related experiences. Ideas stick when they are anchored on shared experiences.

This book has Rob's philosophy, and that of many other entrepreneurs, in mind. Over the past decade my team and I have embarked on a comprehensive research study to uncover best practices, collect stories, and validate how small- and mid-sized companies are growing Sticky Brands. Since 2005 we have interviewed over 1,000 CEOs and business owners, 5,000 sales and marketing professionals, and profiled over 750 companies.

This book combines my professional experience developing and implementing brand strategies with the stories of successful mid-market companies to create a comprehensive guide on how you can grow a Sticky Brand.

Your Sticky Branding Playbook

This book is action oriented.

I see no point writing a business book that is consumed and forgotten. This is your branding playbook. Take the ideas and stories discussed in the book and apply them to your business.

The book has a modular design. There are four sections that feature the 12 Principles of a Sticky Brand, as well as a concluding half-Principle at the end. Each Principle is a guide to help you make your business stand out, attract customers, and drive sales.

Part 1 focuses on positioning your business — where to play, how to win, and how to describe what you do. Part 2's focus is on differentiation — how to stand out like an orange tree in an evergreen forest. Part 3 discusses the principles of sales, creating demand for your products and services so that you become your customers' first choice. And Part 4 looks inside your business, guiding you to grow your brand from the inside out.

You can read the book cover to cover, or you can read each Principle or Part on its own. The book is set up for you to use, reference, and apply as needed.

At the end of each chapter you will find a short exercise that will guide you through applying the concepts to your business. The exercises are designed to spark thought, introspection, and conversation. Companies with Sticky Brands have a great deal of self-awareness and invest time and resources into understanding their customers, market, and what it takes to stand out and have a recognizable brand.

This book is a guide to growing your brand. It provides the concepts, processes, and questions you need to analyze your business and take the necessary steps to grow a Sticky Brand.

Your customers are waiting. They are craving a company like yours to challenge the status quo and deliver them the products, services, and experiences they appreciate. It takes leadership. Take the first step and commit to growing your company into a Sticky Brand. This is your playbook to guide you on that journey.

The 12.5 Principles of a Sticky Brand

Part 1: Position to Win

Sticky Brands play to win. They focus all their expertise and resources on where they play, who they serve, and how they deliver value to their customers. Customers choose Sticky Brands first because they are simply better.

Principle 1: Simple Clarity

Simple Clarity is the ability to simply and succinctly describe your business, what makes it unique, and who it serves. Simple Clarity is about speaking in the language of your customers, and clearly explaining your company's story.

Simple Clarity is the foundation of a Sticky Brand. When you achieve it your business becomes more findable, referable, memorable, and desirable.

Principle 2: Tilt the Odds

Sticky Brands Tilt the Odds in their favor because they are not all things to all people. They choose where to play and how they will win to create a sustainable competitive advantage.

Tilt the Odds for your company by focusing on niche markets or services where it stands out as the first choice.

Principle 3: Function That Resonates

Function That Resonates is the pursuit of delivering value-added services that resonate with your customers. Customers want substance over flash and will seek out companies who truly understand them and their needs.

What do your customers really want? Identify how you can evolve your services to deliver measurable results for your clients.

Part 2: Authentic Differentiation

Sticky Brands don't behave like faceless companies. They stand out because they reveal their personality, share their opinions, and build real customer relationships.

Principle 4: Engage the Eye

Sticky Brands are visual brands. They engage their customers' eyes because they know their customers judge them based on what they see. Sight is the most important human sense for evaluating brands and making purchase decisions.

Build a strong visual identity for your brand that engages your customers' eyes and lets them know your business is unique.

Principle 5: Total Customer Experience

Sticky Brands are built on a collection of experiences. It doesn't matter what the company promotes, it's what the customers experience that counts. The experience shapes the perception of the brand. Sticky Brands provide their customers with compelling experiences that keep them coming back.

Find what makes your business unique and better, and bake that into the customer experience.

Principle 6: "That's Interesting. Tell Me More."

The five best words you can hear a customer say are, "That's interesting. Tell me more." If you can get them to say that, you have caught their attention and they will listen to what you have to say.

Sticky Brands cut through the clutter of their market and engage their customers with Brand Storylines — stories that engage them in a conversation and build relationships.

Part 3: Punch Outside Your Weight Class

Sticky Brands stand out in their industry. They can compete and win against the big guys, because they're not afraid to blow their own horns. Make your brand so visible and engaging that it's hard to ignore.

Principle 7: First Call Advantage

Sticky Brands are their customers' first call when they are ready to buy. It's a powerful sales position. A First Call Advantage sets customer expectations, and provides an opportunity to solve their needs before they shop anywhere else.

Build relationships with your market — prospects, customers, and referral partners — upwards of three years before they need your services.

Principle 8: Be Everywhere

Sticky Brands just seem to be everywhere. They have a buzz about them that's usually the domain of much larger companies. Unlike the big guys, they don't spend outrageous amounts of money on marketing and advertising. They stand out by growing a community.

Grow a community around your brand. Build and scale relationships so your brand is everywhere.

Principle 9: Pick Your Priorities

The number one value of growing a Sticky Brand is sales. Sticky Brands sell more, faster — provided they are purposeful with their resources. Small- and mid-sized companies don't have vast marketing budgets and resources to move the sales needle.

To drive sales and grow a Sticky Brand, focus on one priority at a time: Volume, Velocity, or Value.

Part 4: Over Commit, Over Deliver

Sticky Brands are deeply committed to the performance of their products and services and the results they deliver. That focus on client results empowers their teams to go above and beyond the call of duty.

Principle 10: Branding from the Inside Out

Sticky Brands are built from the inside out. Their people, culture, and values all come together to foster innovation and deliver remarkable client experiences.

Your company's people, culture, and values are the glue that holds it together. Those strong bonds enable your company to attract the right employees and serve your clients even better.

Principle 11: Proud to Serve

The people who grow Sticky Brands are filled with pride. They take a great deal of pride in their work, their customers, and the results they deliver. And it shows. They cultivate adoring customers because they are deeply committed to the work they do.

Pride is powerful. It propels your company to innovate and deliver exceptional services.

Principle 12: Big Goals and Bold Actions

Sticky Brands make Big Goals and take Bold Actions. Their goals energize the brand. They create momentum and excitement around a business that is infectious. People are excited to talk about the company, refer others to it, and buy from it, because of its accomplishments.

Ratchet up the energy and excitement in your company with Big Goals and Bold Actions.

Principle 12.5: Choose Your Brand

Sticky Brands are built by people: ambitious, impatient, talented people. People who are not satisfied with the status quo or growing just another business. Sticky Brands are built by people who commit to growing them.

Choose your brand. Grow a brand that stands out in your industry like an orange tree in an evergreen forest.

Part 1: Position to Win

No company can be all things to all people and still win, so it is important to understand which where-to-play choices will best enable the company to win.

— *A.G. Lafley, former chairman and CEO of Procter & Gamble, and Roger Martin, dean of Rotman School of Management*[4]

No one ever said business has to be fair. Every company is trying to find a strategy or competitive advantage that positions its brand to win. A company can Tilt the Odds so customers choose it first. Sticky Brands are positioned to win by being clear about what they do, who they serve, and what makes them unique.

In this section you will learn how to:

- Achieve **Simple Clarity** by defining your company in simple, clear language.
- Choose a niche to **Tilt the Odds** in your company's favor by picking a market where your company is perceived as the leader.
- Find **Function That Resonates** with your customers by creating value-added services that deliver measurable client results.

Principle 1: Simple Clarity

Simple Clarity is the ability to simply and succinctly describe your business, what makes it unique, and who it serves. Simple Clarity is about speaking in the language of your customers, and clearly explaining your company's story.

Simple Clarity is the foundation of a Sticky Brand. When you achieve it your business becomes more findable, referable, memorable, and desirable.

Customers Buy from You When They Get You

Your customers are crying out for clarity.

We live in a cluttered world. We have so many options it's hard to sort them out. We've filled our lives with stuff: smartphones, tablets, email, Twitter, Facebook, work, home, kids, soccer practice, projects, vacations … the list goes on. As a result, the average North American is feeling rushed, hurried, and short of time.

Customers do not have time to sort out what your service is or what makes it different. They don't have the bandwidth or interest to learn about your business and build relationships with your employees. They just want to get to the facts and work with a company that makes their lives just a little bit easier.

Surprisingly few companies make their brand easy to understand. They struggle to explain their business clearly. You visit their websites and leave confused. You read their brochures, watch their videos, review their case studies, and after all that you still may not know what they do. Clearly articulating who you are and what you do is easier said than done — especially if your company is innovating and challenging the status quo.

Innovation is the great disrupter of Simple Clarity. You want to package the essence of your business, but also convey what makes it unique and exciting. But how do you explain all this without giving a speech or writing an essay?

The ability to express what your company does simply and succinctly separates average companies from Sticky Brands. It positions your brand to win. The companies that work to combine innovation with Simple Clarity stand out. Simple Clarity demonstrates that a firm is confident in what it is and what it does, and its customers clearly get it.

Just by getting your story clear your brand will become more findable, referable, memorable, and desirable.

The simplicity of your explanation will make it obvious to everyone what your business does, and that instills confidence in your brand. Customers will beat a path to your door because they get you. They are happy to refer you, and they have the language to explain what makes your company unique.

A brand radiates once it achieves Simple Clarity, but finding the words is a process.

Find the Words That Stick

I have wrestled with finding Simple Clarity in every company and service I've launched. I thrash around trying out different ideas, explanations, and metaphors to find the ones that resonate with my market. And I don't let go until I find it.

The largest hurdle in repositioning LEAPJob was finding Simple Clarity. The rebrand was a lot of work with a lot of moving parts, but none of the changes moved the sales needle until we could simply and succinctly explain who we were, what we did, and who we served.

The main issue with repositioning LEAPJob was the word "recruiter." We hated that word. It was packed with negative connotations and industry expectations. For example, people commonly call recruiters "headhunters" or "bounty hunters," and many perceive recruiters as opportunistic and unprofessional.

We weren't headhunters; we were professionals. I wanted to separate our firm from the herd. We refused to call ourselves recruiters. I attempted to eliminate the words "recruiter" and "recruiting" from all of our sales and marketing material and show that we offered high-end services and had exceptional client relationships.

I tried to find a sexier, more sophisticated way to position our services. I tried saying we were "search consultants" or "talent acquisition specialists." I tried to play up the concept of talent management, and emphasize how we improved our clients' performance through people.

I tested my elevator pitches on prospects, clients, and at networking events, and I hit wall after wall. I got puzzled looks when I said, "LEAPJob is a talent management agency. We help our clients find and attract the best sales talent." A few would say, "What does that mean?" But most people would smile and nod, make pleasant conversation, and move on. My attempt to displace "recruiter" from our description was falling flat.

My "a-ha moment" came when I was analyzing our website statistics in Google Analytics. I kept noticing three words that appeared in our keyword reports: "sales," "recruiter," and "Toronto." We had never paired any of these words, but I noticed a pattern. Companies were searching "sales recruiter Toronto" to find a sales recruiter based in Toronto.

When I discovered how our customers were searching for our services, the lights turned on. I could clearly explain my business quickly and easily, "LEAPJob is a sales recruiter based in Toronto, Canada. We help our clients find and attract the right sales talent." That's it. That was my elevator pitch. I didn't need a fancy value proposition or an explanation of how we delivered our services. I simply needed to share the facts in the language of my customers.

We updated our website, marketing materials, and sales pitches, and within weeks our phones started ringing. We had achieved Simple Clarity.

Once we knew what people were looking for, we made our website really easy to find. We went through every page on our site and optimized each page for the phrases "sales recruiter Toronto" and "sales recruiting Toronto." Within ninety days we started receiving inquiries. That was a first. Up until then our website had simply functioned as an online brochure. By embedding our Simple Clarity into our website, the phone started ringing all the time with people looking for our services.

Inquiries from our website accounted for 50 percent of LEAPJob's sales. If someone was looking to hire a salesperson in the Toronto area, LEAPJob came up at the top of the list. And because we worked to make our website sell as well as our best salesperson, the opportunities poured in.

The positioning worked equally well in the real world. We had the answer when someone asked, "What do you do?" We simply said, "We're sales recruiters." And if we were outside of the Toronto area, we'd let the prospect know that we were geographically focused. The positioning statement was simple and concise, and it helped our market categorize our services.

That's the power of Simple Clarity. It makes your brand easier to talk about, easier to remember, and easier to find. The right words make all the difference in the world.

A good way to think about Simple Clarity for your brand is that it's like adding a label to a file folder in your customers' minds. The label doesn't provide a list or detailed notes of the folder's contents, it's a reference point. It's a basic tool to help your customers identify your brand and file it away so they can retrieve it easily later. And the clearer the label, the easier it is for your customers to categorize, store, and retrieve.

For a label to be useful it should be three things:

1. Short: Ideally ten words or less.
2. Descriptive: The label offers an explanation of the contents.
3. Memorable: Easy to find and easy to remember.

Simple Clarity follows the same principles. Describe your business in ten words or less using the language of your customers. Use a description that is easy to remember and easy to categorize for later reference. That's it.

LEAPJob used "sales recruiter Toronto." It's a clear label, and in three words we achieved Simple Clarity.

Don't Make Me Think

Crafting a compelling elevator pitch is one of the primary sources of brand confusion. We have been taught that we need a compelling pitch to stand out — something that will get us noticed and create interest in forty-five seconds or less (the length of time it takes to ride an elevator).

The challenge is that we tinker too much. To find something that pops, we play with the words, metaphors, and analogies. We can get too creative. We use words and phrases that make people think, and that can lead to confusion.

Thinking slows down our ability to retain information. Most of the time our brain is working on autopilot. We don't focus on every decision we make because that would slow us down into a state of analysis paralysis. Rather, we only dive into the very interesting or very important decisions.

Dr. Richard Perloff writes in *The Dynamics of Persuasion* that people process information in two modes: centrally and peripherally. He explains, "When people process information centrally, they carefully evaluate message arguments, ponder implications of the communicator's ideas, and relate to their own knowledge and values."[5]

Central thinking is when we are deeply engaged in an idea or decision. We seek out all the facts and information we can on the topic. In a buying cycle, this level of thought takes place when you are evaluating your options and making the final decision.

Think back to your last major purchase. Did you go into analysis overdrive to make sure you were making the right decision? Did you use Google to find and consume all the reviews, fact sheets, and data you could find? This level of analysis is central thinking. You are using your full brain to make better decisions.

Central thinking requires a lot of cognitive energy, and we cannot sustain this level of thinking for long. After a while our brain has to let go and let us get on with our day-to-day lives. This is where peripheral thinking comes into play.

Dr. Perloff continues, "When processing peripherally, people invariably rely on simple decision making rules or heuristics. For example, an individual may invoke a heuristic that 'experts are to be believed' and, for this reason (and this reason only), accept the speaker's recommendation."

"Heuristics" is a term commonly used in the science of persuasion. It means a rule of thumb, and it functions as a mental shortcut. We look to cues to find a larger story or meaning. For example, in business we often refer to the "80/20 Rule," which implies 80 percent of your sales come from 20 percent of your customers. This rule of thumb is a heuristic; it helps us make connections quickly. Our peripheral thinking relies heavily on heuristics because it enables us to interpret a story with a few suggestions from the communicator.

Advertisers play extensively with our peripheral thinking. We infer a person is a doctor if she is wearing a white lab coat and has a stethoscope. An advertiser can make an actor look like a doctor just by giving her the right outfit. This is a heuristic. It is a visual shorthand that quickly conveys a lot of information and supports our desire for rapid decision making.

We live the bulk of our lives peripherally processing information. The products we choose, the foods we eat, the people we work with, and the vendors we select are all preconditioned. It's far easier to go with what we know than to centrally consider each and every decision. "Contemporary society, with its multiple stimuli, unfathomably complex issues, and relentless social change, makes it inevitable that people will rely on mental shortcuts much of the time," writes Dr. Perloff. Only the most important decisions or the most stimulating ideas are centrally processed.

Simple Clarity is effective because it plays to our need for mental shortcuts. Fluffing up an elevator pitch waters down Simple Clarity because it triggers our central thinking. The facts are far easier to remember and share than a creative play on words. Rather than taxing your customers' minds, help them quickly and easily qualify your brand, and file it away for later.

The Three Types of Simple Clarity

The foundation of a Sticky Brand is how well you can describe your business. Without any fluff, pomp, or buzzwords, describe your business. Do your customers get it? Is it easy to remember and easy to refer? Can you explain it to someone outside of your industry so they get it too?

As you get clarity in your answers, you want to push the description of your business even further. You want to share your story so that it makes your company stand out and easy to remember.

Simple Clarity descriptions can be focused on the most important aspect of your business, the one that your customers will most relate to. There are three potential areas of your business that Simple Clarity can cover. They are your company's:

- *Category*: What is your company's specialty?
- *Function*: What does your company do?
- *Situation*: Who does your company serve?

Category: What Is Your Company's Specialty?

Category descriptions are most common for companies with a clear niche or focus. Clearly stating what your business specializes in can be a differentiator. For example, LEAPJob's Simple Clarity used the Category description, "sales recruiter Toronto." The phrase states the company's niche.

Another example is Deighton Associates Limited, a software firm with a global reach. The company is Positioned to Win by focusing on a niche. Deighton is a primary supplier of software systems for Departments of Transportation (DOT) around the world. Its flagship product, dTIMS, manages the DOT's assets: pavements, bridges, culverts, guardrails, signs, and water infrastructure.

According to Vicki Deighton, CEO of Deighton Associates, "Our clients are global. Over 40 percent of the U.S. State DOTs use our system. We have seven out of nine provinces in South Africa, and over 50 percent of the available market in Australia. One hundred percent of the roads you drive on in New Zealand are run on our product." Deighton also has a substantial footprint in Europe.

Deighton has a clear niche, and its strategy is to go deeper and wider within this market. Its Simple Clarity is "total infrastructure asset management software." This demonstrates to the market what Deighton is, what it does, and what expertise it has to offer. The company is clear about its positioning.

Deighton's Simple Clarity has not been static. Vicki explains, "Deighton was founded in 1986 in response to an industry demand for solutions in the pavement management industry. We grew a very strong customer base and partner network in the sector, and became known as pavement management experts. As we grew with our clients they called us in to manage more of their assets: culverts, water, signs, etcetera. We worked closely with our clients and partners, and evolved our brand into 'total infrastructure asset management experts.' Since the early 2000s, the Deighton brand has extended beyond pavement into all infrastructure assets in a department of transportation or a large industrial company."

Deighton uses Simple Clarity purposefully to position itself, and it evolves the statement as necessary. In the eighties and nineties Deighton called itself "pavement management experts," but for the past ten years it has been "infrastructure asset management experts."

Clearly defining what you do provides focus. Deighton uses its positioning to focus its strategy, marketing, and product development. The company continually asks itself, "What does total infrastructure asset management mean?" And that acts as a beacon for the management team to make purposeful decisions.

Like all growing firms Deighton finds opportunities outside of its niche, but they come back to their Simple Clarity again and again to determine if an opportunity is a fit.

Function: What Does Your Company Do?

In large or highly competitive industries a Category description is not effective.

Cardinal Couriers, for example, would be lost in their industry with a Category description. Cardinal is a regional courier that specializes in making deliveries before 8:00 a.m. Its global competitors describe themselves as couriers and logistics companies, but Cardinal Couriers differentiates itself by using its Function as a description. Cardinal's Simple Clarity states what it does: "pre-8:00 a.m. delivery."

Pre-8:00 a.m. delivery is not necessarily new. Courier companies like UPS and FedEx offer it, but they treat it as a premium service. They charge prohibitively expensive rates and encourage their customers to use standard delivery options. Cardinal is redefining the category, because pre-8:00 a.m. delivery is its core expertise. When most companies are shutting down for the day, Cardinal is getting ramped up — it works best at night.

The service is pretty remarkable. Cardinal makes all of its deliveries before its clients show up to work in the morning. A customer either uses a Cardinal Vault, which is a storage locker for their deliveries, or they provide Cardinal with key access to their facilities after-hours. For example, Cardinal works with many of the automotive companies delivering parts to dealerships. When a dealer places an order for a part, it is received by the automotive company and then processed using Cardinal's warehouse and delivery services. The Cardinal driver has a key to the dealership's garage, and they leave the delivery in a predefined spot so it is ready for installation the next day. This is very convenient for the dealership, because the parts are available the next day and the delivery service doesn't disturb the business operations.

Companies love Cardinal for its convenience, reliability, and cost. Even though similar delivery options are available from the global couriers, Cardinal can offer an even better service for two to three times less. They achieve this by focusing their expertise, and creating client density along its shipping routes to maximize efficiency and reduce costs.

Cardinal's service has evolved over thirty-five years, and can be clearly tied to its origins. The company started out shipping parts to farmers — if a farmer's tractor broke down in the field, Cardinal's drivers would bring the part right to the tractor and leave it in the cab. As the company grew, it added "vaults" to its routes. A farmer could install a vault near their fields, and the Cardinal driver would leave the parts in the vault before 8:00 a.m. the next day. The vault system was convenient for the customer, and efficient for Cardinal.

Cardinal's pedigree led it to develop a set of core skills and assets: nighttime operations, customer density in rural areas, and a vault system for delivering parts and products outside of business hours. These capabilities allowed Cardinal to create a niche in the courier industry. It's not marketing hype, it's operational excellence they are selling.

Cardinal's Simple Clarity is rooted in its origins and its core skills and assets. They have unique capabilities to offer their customers, and "pre-8:00

a.m. delivery" acts as the foundation of their brand — it's what they do. A Function description differentiates the brand from the giants of their sector.

Situation: Who Does Your Company Serve?

Companies can also create Simple Clarity by being really clear about who they work with. Situation descriptions go a step beyond the Category and Function descriptions, and provide a set of guidelines about who the company will work with.

Quarry Integrated Marketing, for example, does not fit nicely into a description of Category or Function. It is a marketing communications agency that works with companies that are marketing technical products and services. For example, Quarry launched the Subaru Outback in Canada and the BlackBerry in North America.

The challenge to finding Quarry's Simple Clarity is that a simple three- to five-word statement does not encapsulate its focus. Instead, the company uses a set of qualifying statements to describe its positioning. Quarry is a marketing communications agency, and it specializes in working with technical or engineered products. It focuses on companies experiencing a marketplace disruption, or striving for significant growth. And it targets accounts that will invest greater than one hundred thousand dollars in billings per year.

Quarry packages the qualifying statements with stories and prose, but the essence is clear. The company knows what it is, who it works with, and where it delivers the most value.

Quarry's positioning accelerates its sales process because it functions as a checklist. The company specifies what it is and what it does, and its account managers ask if a prospect fits these criteria. When they engage a prospect, they use probes to qualify if the client is a good fit for them:

- Are you looking for a marketing communications agency?
- Do you need an agency with proven expertise in engineered and technical products and services?
- Is your market experiencing a shift or a transformation?
- Do you invest over one hundred thousand dollars in external marketing services?

If a prospect fits all four criteria, there is a foundation to do good work together. If not, both parties can move on. It's that simple.

For example, Quarry works with John Deere. A creative ad on a billboard or in a magazine is not going to sell a three-hundred-thousand-dollar Deere combine. The products are complex and technical and require human intervention to sell. Deere relies on rich marketing material, messaging, and branding to support its sales efforts — the type of expertise and services Quarry provides. Deere and Quarry can quickly qualify each other based on Quarry's Simple Clarity. The relationship gets off on the right foot because both companies know from the start that they are a fit for each other.

Situation descriptions are the most complex form of Simple Clarity, and they can be problematic. They don't adhere nicely to the label-on-a-file-folder principle, and they're not always easy to remember. Quarry can lead with a Category description, but to generate effective referrals it needs to include the target market, desired outcomes, and size of account in its description. With some wordsmithing it can be made to fit onto a label, but the Situational description tends to be more useful. It's easier to work with four Situational questions than a carefully worded statement.

Situation descriptions work best in well-defined markets with educated buyers. They tend to be the domain of service providers selling big ticket items with average size sales over one hundred thousand dollars. The complexity of the service and the buying process provides the firm a little bit more time to articulate who they are, what they do, and who they serve. Its customers are more inclined to be centrally thinking, as opposed to peripherally thinking, and more willing to take the time to consider the nuances of each firm and what makes it unique.

Make Your Brand Findable, Referable, Memorable, and Desirable

Simple Clarity makes it easy for your customers to categorize your brand, file it away for later, and refer to it when they have a need.

It takes work. Simple Clarity is one of the hardest Principles to master because it requires analysis and testing. You have to dig into the varying aspects of your business, find the essence of your brand, and distill it into a simple, short description — which is easier said than done. But the effort is worthwhile. No other Principle will move the sales needle more than achieving Simple Clarity for your brand.

When your brand is easy to find, easy to remember, and easy to refer to, it becomes more desirable. It demonstrates the brand is credible, and propels customers to choose it first.

Exercise: Simple Clarity

Objective:

In the language of your customers, describe your brand in ten words or less.

You Are, You Do, You Serve

The foundation of a Simple Clarity statement is answering three questions about your business:

- Who is your company?
- What does it do?
- Who does it serve?

Try to craft those three answers into a short statement that describes your business. Don't fret if it's longer than ten words. Focus on clarity first. Get to the facts, you can refine and distill your statement afterward.

Does It Sell?

A Simple Clarity description may look great on paper, but it does not carry much value until you get real customer feedback. The best way to test your Simple Clarity descriptions are to use them. Go out and sell. It's amazing what you can discover in a sales call if you are listening.

Pay attention to how people respond to your Simple Clarity statement. Ask yourself:

- **Did it resonate?** What statements, facts, figures, or stories resonated with the individual? What worked well?
- **Did you face objections?** Did the statement cause confusion or objections? Did the individual express any complaints, issues, or challenges?
- **What did they ask?** What questions did you receive? Did they ask for more details at any point?

Every time you share your Simple Clarity description is a learning opportunity. Keep track of your responses. You will gain insight after a single pitch, but the real gold is found when you have delivered it five to ten times. This is when you start to see patterns, and this knowledge is invaluable in developing and refining your Simple Clarity descriptions.

The market will tell you when you have Simple Clarity. Listen.

Principle 2: Tilt the Odds

Sticky Brands Tilt the Odds in their favor because they are not all things to all people. They choose where to play and how they will win to create a sustainable competitive advantage.

Tilt the Odds for your company by focusing on niche markets or services where it stands out as the first choice.

Avoid the Soft, Squishy Middle

Operating in the middle of your industry is not a happy place, but it's where many companies get trapped. They lack the economies of scale of the big companies, and don't have the nimbleness and low overhead of the smaller players. The middle is the worst of both worlds.

The middle presents significant disadvantages for growing your brand too. In the middle you are "the other guys," and run the risk of not being perceived as the best. Bob Spiers, CEO of ProVision IT believes, "Clients look for certainty of delivery. It's a matter of trust. Any firm can deliver a one-off service, but brands are grown by consistently achieving and exceeding expectations."

ProVision IT is a mid-sized IT staffing firm based in Toronto, Canada. They help big companies staff their IT projects with contract and full-time employees. The company's clients are typically large institutions like the banks, federal and local governments, insurance and telecommunication companies — the sorts of companies with large IT departments and with big budgets and complex needs. ProVision IT's role is to provide the talent that work in these departments.

Bob continues, "Our largest competitors are typically global staffing firms. Their brands signal large, established, credible, and stable." Companies seek out the big guys, because there is an expectation of consistent delivery — their services just work. Clients may forego innovation and new ideas for a safe, reliable option.

IBM capitalized on this phenomenon in the seventies and eighties with the phrase, "No one ever got fired for buying IBM." The big name signals trust and reliability. Ironically, IBM coined the phrase to support their strategy for creating what they called FUD — fear, uncertainty, and doubt — in its competitors' products. IBM's goal was to insert an expectation in its customers' minds that big is better, because big is safe.

The fear, uncertainty, and doubt generated by the big guys leaves a negative film on the companies competing in the middle of an industry. They are perceived as the backup option. They don't have the credibility of the big stalwarts, and they don't have the bespoke, customer relationships of the little guys. The middle companies are rarely the first choice of customers.

"You have to give your clients a clear reason to work with you," continues Bob. "The large competitors demonstrate credibility in their size. We have to differentiate ourselves not only in our performance and our people, but in how our brand is perceived."

Perception is a major issue in the middle. A company stuck in the middle may offer a superior service, but it has to fight harder to sell it. It has to explain why it is different more often, and work even harder to prove it. According to John Philip Jones, an advertising researcher and professor at Newhouse School, smaller brands have to spend disproportionately more than larger brands to achieve the same level of recognition.

Adam Morgan writes in *Eating the Big Fish*, "Brand Leaders make more damn money than we do."[6] He demonstrates that a brand leader — a company that dominates a category — makes triple the profit of a number-two brand. A number-three brand makes half the profit of a number-two. He says, "If profit allows a company to make choices, to invest resources in finding sources of future competitive advantage, then this disparity serves to widen the discrepancy between the chips the Brand Leader has at its disposal and the pile we have to play with."

That doesn't mean all is lost for smaller companies. To compete and win against the large, stalwart brands requires competing on your own terms. The challenge is not size or resources, it's where you will play and how you will win. When you are competing with companies that are dominant players in your industry, you've got to Tilt the Odds by finding new ways to compete and win.

Own Your Niche

It's easy to get lost in the shuffle when you are a generalist. Peter Reaume, CEO of National Logistics Services (NLS) explains, "Prior to purchasing NLS in 2006, my company Logisti-Solve was doing a bit of everything: entertainment, healthcare, food, and pharmaceuticals. We were growing by 30 percent year-over-year, but we had no brand. It wasn't sustainable. We were not experts in anything."

National Logistics Services is the leading logistics provider for fashion, footwear, and apparel companies. The company manages the full logistics process, from purchase order to delivery, as well as distribution, inventory management, e-commerce, and reverse logistics for recalls and returns. It has established a niche in its industry, and is positioned as the clear market leader. NLS has a who's who of clients: Adidas, Under Armour, Ann Taylor, Coach, Loft, New Balance, and Aeropostale, to name a few.

But NLS started as a generalist. Logistics is an industry that gravitates toward the middle — serving any and all clients. At the core, logistics companies have trucks, technology, and warehouses to move goods — it doesn't really matter what's in the boxes or on the skids, as long as there is room on the trucks. This flexibility and adaptability of the service leads to a branding problem. What are you known for?

Generalists can compete on three factors:

- Price
- Availability
- Relationships

When a market is growing and booming, generalists can ride the wave and be successful. Peter's prior company, Logisti-Solve, rode the entertainment wave. In the nineties CDs and DVDs were a strong business, and Logisti-Solve worked with the major entertainment companies and music retailers. The entertainment industry crashed when Apple released the iPod and iTunes in 2001 and the sale of CDs and DVDs in brick-and-mortar stores plummeted.

Shifts or downturns in a sector can be catastrophic for generalists and leave them competing solely on price. And selling on price sucks! It's a perpetual race to the bottom. There is always someone willing to sell for a little bit less. The only companies that benefit from selling on price are the big stalwarts of an industry. The experience taught Peter the value of growing a Sticky Brand, and the importance of growing a brand in a niche that you can defend and own — which is a tenet for positioning your brand to win.

The decision to focus on a niche was very purposeful, and it took a lot of work, investment, and sacrifice for NLS to own their niche. "It was one of the scariest things I've ever done," says Peter. "We knew we had to specialize, but the transition was hard." However, it turned out to be more than worth it.

National Logistics Services has a long, storied past. The company was founded in 1967 as the fulfillment arm of Dylex. Dylex was one of North America's largest retailers in the last decades of the twentieth century, and managed major retail brands such as Tip Top Tailors, Thriftys, Bi-Way, and Fairweather. At its peak, the company operated 2,700 stores across seventeen chains in Canada and the United States.[7] NLS was the logistics arm that managed these stores, as well as provided logistics services to a broad range of external customers. In 2000 Dylex went into bankruptcy protection and sold several of their businesses, including NLS, to American Eagle Outfitters.

In 2006 American Eagle sold NLS to Logisti-Solve. They were a much smaller logistics company, but the purchase made sense for Peter and his team. NLS had highly trained people, proprietary technology, and excellent processes. Peter saw a team that could do great things, but their challenge was focus.

After the purchase of NLS, Peter and his team made a commitment to specialize. They analyzed their core skills and assets, their market, and where their industry was headed, and found an opportunity: fashion and footwear. The company already had deep roots and expertise in the retail industry from their history with Dylex and American Eagle Outfitters. In addition, fashion, footwear, and apparel are complex industries, and many logistics firms shy away from them. "Footwear and fashion are problematic, because there are a lot of products that are changing constantly. Each season brings new products. Some products do really well, and manufacturers like Under Armour and Adidas ramp up to serve that demand. And other products fail, and are abandoned just as quickly," explains Peter.

NLS recognized this was a niche they could own. It's complex. There are clear barriers to entry, and to excel in the niche requires specific core skills and assets. And there weren't many competitors focused on the niche at the time. NLS could define their niche and position its brand as the de facto leader of the category. NLS could Tilt the Odds away from being trapped in the middle as generalists to the brand leader of a niche market.

Tilting the Odds Requires Sacrifice

Being opportunistic and being all things to all people is the easy route. It is easy to chase the opportunity in front of you versus specializing and saying "no" to opportunities that don't fit.

Many companies experience a terrifying lull after they commit to a niche. A niche strategy requires sacrifice and commitment. Once you commit to the niche you cannot take on the generalist or opportunistic work outside of your specialty, because that will dilute your market position. It also takes time to ramp up the sales and marketing to bring on new customers in the niche, and get back up to full productivity.

National Logistics Services went through eighteen months of sales purgatory to secure its niche. The company set its strategy and made a commitment to specialize in fashion and footwear. The change was communicated to clients, and sales and marketing focused on fashion and footwear brands, as the company transitioned away from the customers that did not fit with its new service.

NLS went all in, completely rebranding the company for its new niche. Peter explains, "Prior to the change we had a generic website focused on trucks, material handling equipment, and conveyors. We looked like any logistics company. We had to demonstrate to our target market that we had a passion for the goods they were marketing.

"We scrapped the old marketing material, and came back with the kind of materials you would expect for a retailer or a major fashion brand. We didn't talk about trucks. We talked about clothing and e-commerce, and the topics that mattered to our target market." NLS updated its website and marketing material to speak in the language of its customers. The company achieved Simple Clarity with its words, and its marketing material presented a forward-thinking company committed to fashion, footwear, and apparel.

But all they heard was silence. Eighteen months of crickets.

National Logistics Services' transition to Tilt the Odds would have tested the intestinal fortitude of the strongest companies. The company went eighteen months with virtually no new sales and operated with reduced revenue because of the clients it had transitioned away from. And the company did this with over 250 employees. All Peter and his leadership team could do was wait, communicate, and have faith in their strategy.

It was a painful period and NLS was forced to make significant cutbacks and sacrifices. The company offered early retirement packages, which some employees accepted, and made layoffs across the board, from senior managers to frontline staff. Peter, or a member of the leadership team, met with each person who was laid off during the transition and explained the situation, "We spread the cuts across the entire organization, but we also made a commitment to every person we laid off. We told each and every employee, 'We want you back.'

"To get through the jittery period we over-communicated. We told everyone it was a tough period, but the right strategy. We reiterated the message every single month, and at every opportunity we could," continues Peter.

They also defined a Big Goal for the company. Peter declared in 2008 that the company would move back to profitability before his fortieth birthday, which was June 10, 2010. And it did. A few days before Peter's fortieth birthday, NLS turned a corner. It took just one new customer to break them out of sales purgatory, Aeropostale. From there the company rocketed into growth mode. By the end of 2010, NLS had grown by 20 percent, and it has been growing by 30 percent year-over-year since. As well, since June 2010, every month has been profitable.

Almost every employee that was laid off during the transition came back. The NLS management team was true to their word when they said, "We want you back." The caliber of the team was a primary reason Logisti-Solve bought the company, and every person made a major contribution and a major sacrifice to Tilt the Odds for the business. Now the company has over 450 employees and is adding new staff constantly.

Repositioning a company is incredibly painful and challenging, but the experience will leave a lasting mark on the team and the culture. "The experience brought our team closer together, and it's now tighter than ever," says Peter.

The odds are now in National Logistics Services favor. The company has a brand, and it's sticky. NLS has set the bar of service so high in its niche that the major logistics providers have either left the space or avoid direct competition with NLS. The company has a powerful market position, and has positioned itself to win.

Break Through Sales Purgatory

It is not unusual for a company to go through a period of sales purgatory as it Tilts the Odds. It takes sacrifice and commitment to capture a niche market.

My team and I went through a similar period of sales purgatory when we repositioned LEAPJob. We were walking away from fifteen years of specialization in one sector to Tilt the Odds in another. The transition was painful and scary, because our sales plummeted for nine months.

Like NLS, we went all in for our new niche. We transitioned out the clients that didn't fit our specialization and made every effort to refer them to quality suppliers. We invested deeply in our sales and marketing efforts: new website, a PR and media campaign, email newsletters, direct marketing, search engine marketing, and a variety of other tactics that would grow brand awareness. But there was a dip. It takes time to establish your reputation in a new market, build trust, and fill your sales funnel. Tilting the Odds takes a real commitment of time, cash, and resources.

When you Tilt the Odds, expect a period of sales purgatory. It is an inevitable reality of implementing a niche strategy. Be prepared, and treat this process as a Big Goal — see Principle 12 for more insights on Big Goals and Bold Actions.

To make it through sales purgatory you will need four things:

Cash

Cash is an obvious ingredient. What would it mean for your business if you went six, twelve, or twenty-four months with minimal sales? Could you survive? If not, you may not be ready to Tilt the Odds.

Time

Time is always the great unknown. How long will sales purgatory take? Based on my company's research and experience, an average business-to-business sales funnel takes nine months to fill. This is pretty universal across industries that sell products and services that have a sales cycle of two to six months and an average size sale of $10,000 to $100,000. For companies with longer or more complex sales cycles, sales purgatory can take longer. Selling to the government or large institutions that require requests for proposals and drawn-out buying cycles will increase the period of sales purgatory. A good rule of thumb is to predict that sales purgatory will be either nine months, or three times the length of your average sales cycle. Go with whichever timeframe is longer.

Communication

The third ingredient is frequent communications. Peter Reaume recommends "over-communicate." You cannot communicate enough the importance of your firm's strategy, why you are going through this process, and what you will achieve on the other side.

Communicate this message to everyone — your staff, partners, prospects, and customers. And don't let up. Every week work to reiterate your message. This is a period when you can't let up on communicating and keeping everyone abreast of the process, the successes, and even the realities of the situation. Sales purgatory can tear your culture apart if it isn't managed. This is a team effort. If you fail to communicate enough, your team's imaginations can run wild. Rumors can start, and your employees can become disillusioned. Without clear and constant communication your staff can lose their way in sales purgatory.

Celebrations

Finally, you need to celebrate the wins, no matter how small. Weekly team huddles to celebrate the small wins are very effective. They help to keep up the morale. When you have a bigger win, go all out. Throw a party. Make it a celebration. Everyone needs to see the light at the end of the tunnel, and know their hard work is valued.

The more you communicate and celebrate, the stronger your team will be. When you finally break through sales purgatory you will be even stronger for the process. The communication skills, culture, and your team's ability to adapt and change will stick with your company for the long haul.

It's Okay to Say "No"

"No" is not a bad word, but we have been taught to fear it. It's hard to hear "no," and it's even harder to say it. "No" is a defensive word. It is a rejection and it can lead to conflict. Sticky Brands do not avoid the word. Actually, they are Positioned to Win, because they say "no" frequently.

Sticky Brands do not serve all people — they are not one-stop shops. To Tilt the Odds you have to set clear guidelines that explain who you are, what you do, and who you serve.

NLS defined a clear focus for its business. Its niche is logistics services for fashion and footwear brands. Even with all the company's success, it still has to stay focused and prepared to say "no" to customers. "Canadian Tire really liked the work we did with their Forzani division, and asked us to expand into general retail. But managing the logistics of canoes and tires is very different from shoes. It was a big opportunity, but we had to stay true to our strategy and respectfully decline the offer," Peter explains.

Not many companies will walk away from a big sales opportunity, but it is essential if you want to Tilt the Odds and position your brand to win. Generalists ride the waves of the economy, but specialists outperform regardless of market conditions. NLS has clear guidelines for what it does and why that focus is so important.

What are your guidelines? Can you quickly qualify a prospect or a customer in a few short questions? More importantly, are those questions well understood across your organization and adhered to by all of your staff and salespeople?

At LEAPJob we defined three minimum criteria for every client engagement we took on:

1. Hiring Position: Companies hiring sales and marketing professionals that required talent with at least three years' experience.
2. Location: The position was based in Toronto or the surrounding areas.
3. Salary: The position must have a base salary of forty-five thousand dollars per year or more.

The guidelines were designed to quickly qualify if a prospect was a good match for our services. We set a few basic questions to engage a prospect to gather the information up front. Our salespeople were trained to only send contracts to companies that fit these three guidelines. It was a strict rule, and we managed it carefully.

To Tilt the Odds for our business we were looking to create efficiencies in our recruiting practice. One of the challenges of a recruiting agency is being pulled into unique searches with every new client. For example, one day you may be searching for a software engineer and the next day you're looking for an accountant. Each time a recruiting agency takes on a unique search it has to start from scratch to build their database, establish relationships, and hunt for talent.

Our strategy was to break away from always starting from scratch and focus on a set of positions that drew from a standard database of talent. The idea was to be able to present one candidate to five different clients, because they all had similar hiring needs. This created velocity in our inventory and meant we didn't have to interview as many candidates to hit our placement targets (a placement is a completed hiring project, and we were only paid when a candidate was successfully placed).

The guidelines also made our sales force much more efficient. Rather than investing a lot of time trying to understand a prospect, their needs, and the nuances of their project, the salesperson could get to the point. They could share our story, and ask a few pointed questions to determine if we were a match for each other. If the sales reps found there wasn't a match they could politely tell the prospect we were not a fit. This brought our sales success rate up over 90 percent, because we weren't competing as generalists on price and relationship.

You won't create a Sticky Brand without guidelines. They are your shorthand for where your company will play and how it will win.

Every time you take on a client outside of your niche you are stretching and diluting your core skills and assets. This is effectively leveling the playing field and pushing you back into competition with the big guys. The stalwarts of your industry love it when you take on any piece of business, because that pushes your brand back into the soft, squishy middle.

Play to Your Strengths

Chasing business for business' sake is a fool's game. Sticky Brands are strategic — they apply guidelines to their business to Tilt the Odds in their favor. Sticky Brands have rigor in their sales and delivery. They know who they are, what they do, and who they serve, and they rarely deviate from this path. Being focused is their strength. It helps them harness their resources, and commit to markets and customers that truly value their expertise and services.

Tilt the Odds in your company's favor. Choose where you will play and how you will win, and own that niche. Become so good that your value proposition becomes hard to beat.

Exercise: Tilt the Odds

Objective:

Select a niche or service area for your company that you can protect and own, and be your customers' first choice.

Pick the Right Niche

Not all niche markets are equal, and a lot of time and effort can be wasted developing the wrong niche.

When choosing a niche market for your brand, ask these three questions:

Is There a Market?

For a niche marketing strategy to be effective your clients have to perceive a value in it. Look for customers that have clear, identifiable needs, but who are not having their needs met by the options currently available in the market.

Can You Compete and Win?

Who is already serving this market? How do these customers currently solve their problems? Do you have services or expertise that is better than what they already have? Developing a niche market is built on your business's core skills and assets, and your ability to tap into unmet needs.

Can You Defend Your Brand Position?

This is the most important question, because it requires investing in your brand. You have to commit to win. What core skills or assets does your firm have to service the niche market? And how will you invest in them, develop them, and build them up to protect your market?

These three questions get better the more you ask them. The more you can challenge yourself and your team to go deeper into the questions, the better prepared you will be to Tilt the Odds for your brand.

Principle 3: Function That Resonates

Function That Resonates is the pursuit of delivering value-added services that resonate with your customers. Customers want substance over flash and will seek out companies who truly understand them and their needs.

What do your customers really want? Identify how you can evolve your services to deliver measurable results for your clients.

Sticky Brands Just Work

Your company isn't going to grow a Sticky Brand by outspending the big guys. You cannot beat their marketing or advertising budgets. Your company will win because your products and services just work.

Google has grown into one of the most valuable brands in the world. It is ranked number two on both Interbrand's "Best Global Brands 2013"[8] and the BrandZ's "Top 100 Brand Ranking"[9] for 2013. Interbrand wrote in its 2013 report, "Tech-savvy or not, anyone who has continuous, or even intermittent, access to the internet is aware of the brand, and likely a user of at least one of its numerous offerings. Whether through phone, tablet, computer, or car, the brand is ever-present." The report continues, "The company is constantly assessing its products, phasing out services and offerings that are no longer relevant or are simply unprofitable, and introducing new ones. This responsive behavior suggests that Google pays attention to what consumers like and don't like — a big reason why overall sentiment for the brand is positive."

A key point is "Google pays attention to what consumers like and don't like." The company delivers products that are intuitive, easy to use, and just work. Google Search lets you find what you are looking for as you type. Google Maps show you how to get from point A to point B in seconds, and it will give you turn-by-turn directions on a smartphone.

The simplicity and utility of Google's products bring customers back again and again. The company built a brand based on providing tools that just work, and made them widely accessible. The philosophy is equally relevant for small- and mid-sized brands. Do your products and services just work?

Sticky Brands strive for operational excellence. Marketing hype scratches off quickly. It might get you in the door, but if your company can't deliver consistently, your customers are not going to stay around for long.

It's a Matter of Trust

Used cars may be one of the toughest markets to grow a brand. As Jim Gilbert, CEO of Jim Gilbert's Wheels and Deals says, "We're selling four tires and a piece of tin. We have to make the experience better."

Even commoditized markets can stand out and create Function that Resonates. Jim Gilbert's Wheels and Deals has grown into one of the largest independent used car dealerships in Eastern Canada by being clear on what makes them unique: better-quality used cars. Jim explains, "The average independent used car dealer in Canada sells between 200 to 250 cars per year, and have revenues between $3 to $4 million. Wheels and Deals sell over 1,200 cars a year and our sales are over $30 million."

Jim continues, "We've been in business for thirty-four years, but fourteen years ago we changed our philosophy." In 2000 Wheels and Deals became very focused on its customers and its brand, because there was a major shift in their competitive landscape.

Prior to 2000 Wheels and Deals was like all the other independent used car dealers. It carried an inventory of fifteen to twenty cars, and it sold fifteen to twenty cars a month. It was a straightforward business model that everyone in the used car industry tended to follow. But in the late nineties a new dealership with deep pockets and a new philosophy entered the used car market. The new dealer carried an inventory of one hundred cars on its lot and sold one hundred cars per month.

Very quickly the large competitor took market share away from the little guys and created an uneven playing field. Customers were drawn to the choices offered by the larger player and were less inclined to check out the smaller used car dealerships. If Jim and his team were to survive they would have to change their approach.

Jim watched the large competitor and took note of its strengths and weaknesses. He noticed that even though the new dealership offered customers the advantage of greater selection and choice, its employees behaved like "used car salesmen." It wasn't a pleasant buying experience. The sales reps were aggressive, commission driven, and they didn't care what they sold to their customers. Quality be damned. The goal was to sell as many cars as they could.

Jim recognized Wheels and Deals could not compete on inventory at the time, but they could compete on quality and service. A big challenge for people buying a used car is unscheduled maintenance. The car may pass the safety inspection at the time of purchase, but a few months later the car needs new brakes, new tires, or some other unforeseen maintenance issue. Jim Gilbert's Wheels and Deals made a commitment to differentiate their business with better-quality used cars. It was an opportunity to create a new value proposition in the market that would resonate with the company's clientele. It was also a shift in how a used car dealership ran its business, and an area Wheels and Deals could innovate, invest in, and make its own.

Function that Resonates is drawn from an organization's core skills and assets. David Aaker writes in *Managing Brand Equity,*[10] "Assets and skills provide the basis of a competitive advantage that is sustainable.... An asset is something a firm possesses such as a brand name or a retail location, which is superior to that of the competition. A skill is something a firm does better than its competitors, such as advertising or efficient manufacturing."

It's an organization's core skills and assets that enable it to rise above the competition. A company with a Sticky Brand identifies what it does better than anyone else, and then doubles down on that expertise. It distills the specialty, emphasizes it, and enhances it. It makes its core skills and assets an integral part of its business, and an integral part of its value proposition.

When your customers identify with a core skill or asset they will gravitate toward it. They will seek out firms that have unique expertise and choose them first.

Wheels and Deals identified a need for better-quality cars, and it could invest in its core skills and assets to deliver on that promise. Every car Wheels and Deals sells goes through a detailed inspection, and any issues that come up are fixed. The company's mechanics also change the oil, do a brake job, and replace the tires if necessary. The goal is to service the car to at least 250 percent of the government regulations. Wheels and Deals puts its money where its mouth is. The company invests, on average, between $800 and $1,200 in every car.

Jim explains, "We make less money on each car, but we make up for it in volume and customer loyalty." The strategy to sell better cars started out small. Jim knew they could not compete on choice, but the company could deliver a higher quality car. And customers took notice.

Wheels and Deals' customers started coming back again and again and referring their friends and family, because they knew they were buying a hassle-free car. As Wheels and Deals' reputation grew, it attracted more clients, and that gave the company an opportunity to reinvest in the business to grow its inventory — from 15 to 20 cars on the lot to 120 to 130. That reinvestment allowed the company to compete on both quality and choice — a potent combination.

Jim Gilbert's Wheels and Deals grew a Sticky Brand by identifying a clear customer need and innovating to solve it.

Don't Say It, Show It

Marketing can be a cynical game. As soon as one competitor innovates and finds a new value proposition, everyone else starts claiming they do it too. Even if the competition doesn't offer a comparable solution, it is easy for them to spin their marketing to say they do the "same thing."

Wheels and Deals' competitors may claim to offer the same level of quality and follow a similar maintenance process. They can say they are conducting brake jobs, repairs, and detailed inspections, and the consumer wouldn't be the wiser. But there is a difference. The competition services their cars to the government safety standard, while Wheels and Deals services its cars to at least 250 percent of the standard.

Wheels and Deals tackle the marketing deception head on. The company says what it does, shows how it does it, and backs up its claims.

When a new customer visits the Wheels and Deals dealership a sales rep takes them on a tour of the facility. It is situated on six acres of land with a twelve-thousand-square-foot building. The space pops. There's an eye-catching showroom and the staff are friendly. A key stop on the tour is the mechanics' bays. Wheels and Deals have five mechanics' bays, three wash bays, and a team of full-time technicians. The mechanics' bays are unusual for a used car dealership, but an integral part of Wheels and Deals' value proposition. The sales reps show the customer the various facilities, and explain how all of these features make the cars better.

The sales reps also make a point of introducing their customers to the Customer Care Manager. The introduction lets the customer know their purchase will be backed up and there is a real person they can call if they experience any issues — Wheels and Deals provide a ninety-day warranty with each car, and the introduction puts a face on the policy.

The tour is designed to connect the customer with Wheels and Deals' Function That Resonates — sell better-quality cars — and heighten the benefit in the customer's mind. They don't leave it to chance. "Better-quality cars" is reinforced again and again in the facilities, the buying experience, and the support.

The heightened experience sets expectations if the customer visits another dealership. The odds are in Wheels and Deals' favor, because the customer won't get the same experience anywhere else. It positions the company's brand to win.

It's more than a value proposition, it's a process. The customer is working with an organization that delivers a tangible benefit, and they can see it, talk about it, and experience it. Wheels and Deals do not have to sell a unique selling proposition like, "the best-quality used cars." Rather, the whole process delivers that experience. The company is taking its core capabilities and what makes it unique, and radiating that through the entire customer experience. The function resonates, because customers clearly see they are buying a better product.

Results Wanted. What Do Your Services Really Deliver?

You can't have a Sticky Brand without repeat customers. The essence of a Sticky Brand is customers who come back again and again. Part of what brings your customers in the door the first time is a credible solution, but to create repeat customers in a commoditized market, you've got to offer something unique. It takes more than offering an equivalent service to the big guys in your industry. To be Positioned to Win requires innovation. It's a matter of defense.

Theodore Levitt wrote, "People don't want to buy a quarter-inch drill, they want a quarter-inch hole." Levitt's quote is famous because so many companies confuse their corporate purpose. As Jim Gilbert said, "We're selling four tires and a piece of tin." But that's not really what the customer is buying. They are buying a vehicle they will use daily to get to work, take their kids to soccer practice, and travel from point A to point B.

Let's look at another example. The Central Group designs and manufactures point-of-purchase displays and packaging for large consumer brands like Colgate and Nestlé. But that's the drill bits, to paraphrase Levitt. Rick Eastwood, president of The Central Group, is very clear on what his company delivers. He says, "We're not in the business of selling displays and packaging. We're here to help our clients get their products out the door."

Rick points out that manufacturing attractive, functional packaging and displays are table stakes in his industry. Most of his major competitors can deliver a well-designed display. The question is whether or not the display can increase the clients' performance-at-retail or not.

Central's commitment to the end result, "improving performance-at-retail," is what drives them. The company is constantly challenging itself and its clients to quantify and qualify new strategies that improve "performance-in-store." Its view is that a client, the consumer-goods company, isn't simply buying packaging or displays. The client is buying

Figure 3.1: The Central Group ROI Lab. Yes, this is actually the lab, and not a pharmacy. The Central Group has designed the space to create an immersive experience to test a variety of merchandising concepts.

a tool to achieve a tangible retail goal such as launching a new product, increasing category penetration, or differentiating their products from others on the market.

"Improving performance-at-retail" could make an effective tagline and marketing pitch. It is catchy and expresses why consumer-goods companies invest in merchandising programs, but that wouldn't be enough to create Function That Resonates. Central has taken its mission and acted on it. "Improving performance-at-retail" is the company's lens. It gives the team a clear understanding of how their products are used, where they should focus their energies, and keeps them alert for new ideas.

For example, in 2008 Central launched the ROI Lab (see Figure 3.1). The lab enables consumer-goods companies to work with Central's design team to innovate and test categories, packaging, merchandising, and display concepts. It provides insight into actual consumer behaviors and preferences so that Central's clients can determine a marketing concept's effectiveness before it's launched.

Central can set up the space to mimic various retail environments, and conduct research with live shoppers to see how programs will work.

It's a platform to validate retail marketing concepts before they are implemented. The space has a great deal of flexibility and can be designed to re-create a targeted section of a grocery store, pharmacy, or bakery. The ROI Lab enables companies to test products, packaging, and displays on store shelves, and have live customers interact with them. And it helps Central observe consumer behaviors, measure preferences, and determine what works and what doesn't.

When you walk into the lab you are aware it's a lab. The back wall has double-sided mirrors to observe the shopping behaviors, there are cameras embedded in the walls and ceiling, and there are mock checkout lines. The Central Group doesn't try to trick people into thinking they have walked into a grocery store. Central is clear with the participants about what they are testing and what the setting is designed for. It's a place for observation and gleaning consumer attitudes and behaviors to apply the insight.

The ROI Lab has helped Central create a substantial competitive advantage by honing its Function That Resonates. It shifts Central from being considered just another manufacturer to a firm deeply committed to the end result — the customers' results.

Seize Opportunities When They Strike

The ROI Lab has grown substantially since its creation. The original idea was to create a retail showroom to showcase varying merchandising options, and use it as a sandbox to test out ideas. But Central's commitment to the end result took the lab in an unexpected direction.

Rick explains, "The VP of Marketing of a large consumer brand got wind of our lab, and requested a visit." Central was shocked. Why was a large company interested in the lab? Didn't they have their own? It turned out they didn't. The client was interested in testing merchandising options, and it was that little bit of interest that motivated Central's management team to double down on the concept. They studied retail labs from all over the world, established partnerships with key technology providers like IBM, and invested in creating a world-class lab.

Central saw the potential for the ROI Lab because the company has a history and a culture of innovation. In 1990 Central became one of the first high-value-corrugated companies in North America to offer full-color printing. If you purchased a pair of Sorel boots or Bauer skates in the nineties, they came in a box made by The Central Group. But in the early 2000s the company's business shifted. Kaufman Rubber Co., which owned Sorel, went bankrupt, and Bauer moved its manufacturing out of Canada. This was compounded with the downturn in the economy following 9/11, and several other clients faced similar hardships. In a span of eighteen months Central lost almost 60 percent of its business.

The crisis almost destroyed Central, but the tenacity and culture of innovation within the company kicked in. Central studied its market, analyzed its core skills and assets, and determined it could be successful in manufacturing point-of-purchase displays and packaging. Since the low point, the company has grown to over fifty million dollars, and it is on track to grow by another 50 percent in 2015.

It's in Central's DNA to seize opportunities. When the company sees a good idea it doesn't hem and haw and ponder if it should act — it just does it. When a client expressed interest in the ROI Lab, Central seized the opportunity. By creating a retail lab, Central could reinvent its brand once again, shifting from a manufacturer to a strategic partner.

The ROI Lab is only a piece of Central's focus on the end result. The company also developed the Applied Innovation Program, which wraps its clients in data. The program helps clients to reduce costs and boost profitability by providing the data, metrics, and visibility of the supply chain so they can make better decisions. Central works with clients to be very aware, responsive, and accountable to how displays and packaging are used and how they drive in-store retail performance. The belief is that the numbers don't lie.

It takes a lot of commitment to go beyond your core service and consider how your company truly impacts your customers. But when you push yourself and innovate you can create Function That Resonates. Central's approach of wrapping value-added services with their core products clearly differentiates them from the array of manufacturers that sell packaging and displays. The difference is that Central can tell you which displays will work before they are launched. That capability positions their brand to win.

Rick Eastwood describes Central's strategy as "easy in, impossible out."

There is no escaping the relentless march of commoditization. Central would not retain its clients, or acquire new ones, on the ROI Lab alone. It's Central's manufacturing capabilities that get clients in the door, and the company's capabilities and pricing are second to none. Central operates four facilities of over four hundred thousand square feet. It is constantly investing in new equipment, systems, and technology to improve its productivity and capabilities, and it is ISO certified with a deep investment in environmental accreditations.

Central can deliver as well or better than any display manufacturer in North America. This is a basic requirement. If the company loses sight of its cost structures or capacity, it could lose key accounts in a heartbeat. Central is very purposeful in its approach to manufacturing, but, as Rick points out, efficient manufacturing is expected, "Any firm can produce an attractive, cost-effective, and functional corrugated display. The differentiator is: will it work?"

Central makes its brand sticky by offering rich value-added services such as the ROI Lab and the Applied Innovation Program. The company wraps its clients in data and intelligence, and gives them insight they couldn't gain anywhere else. Once the clients begin using the data and research capabilities, they are hooked. Central's relationship shifts from being a supplier of packaging and displays to a strategic partner.

For example, a large consumer-goods brand introduced a new product line to retailers in Canada and they chose to launch it at Central's Innovation Centre. The client brought a different retailer to the Centre each day and used the ROI Lab and boardrooms to demonstrate its products and merchandising strategy. The launch was successful and reinforced Central's relationship with not only the client, but the various retail partners. It demonstrated Central was far more than a manufacturer, it was also a company deeply committed to retail performance. It made Central's brand even stickier.

Many companies avoid focusing on the result because it complicates things. It's easier to sell a commoditized product, because all it takes is fulfilling the customers' requirements for the cheapest price. And it's easier to sell a product if no one is measuring how well it performs. Focusing on the result means your company is raising the bar and making your brand accountable.

Accountability is not for the faint of heart. Challenging your clients to evaluate and change their processes to improve performance means you've got to bring more to the table: more innovation, more data, better talent, and better systems. All of which require more time and investment.

The ROI Lab and Applied Innovation Program have helped Central form a substantial competitive advantage. It shifts the company from a manufacturer of displays to a firm that is deeply committed to the end result — its customers' results.

Make a Commitment

Function That Resonates is a combination of insight, innovation, and operational excellence. You don't create it overnight. It's strategic, it's purposeful, and it takes time. The Central Group and Wheels and Deals were not overnight successes. They improved their services by trying to identify new and better ways to serve their customers. They figured out what their clients were really trying to achieve, and they innovated and focused their services to deliver those results.

When you identify an area that can make a real impact on your clients, hold onto it. Invest in it. Make it your own. Sticky Brands are Positioned to Win, because they have a clear understanding of how they deliver value to clients, and they invest in the operational excellence to deliver on those needs.

Exercise: Function That Resonates

Objective:

Make your products more functional and valuable for your clients by combining them with value-added services.

Discover the Outcomes

Developing Function That Resonates requires a deep understanding of your clients and what they are really trying to achieve. Let's get to the root of your customers' outcomes:

1. On a blank piece of paper, make a list of fifteen customers. If you have multiple products or services with disparate customer segments, focus your list on one segment at a time. Write down the customer's name, what they purchased, and when.
2. Using the Customer Outcomes in the box in Figure 3.2, write next to each customer what they were trying to achieve. Try to get to the root of their purchases. What did the purchase bring them? Entertainment, security, profit, or something else? You can add multiple outcomes to each customer.
3. Count the number of times each outcome occurs on your list. What were the top two or three outcomes? How often do they appear on your list? What does that indicate to you?
4. Look for groupings. Not only count the number of outcomes, but also group them. Outcomes like security, strength, and reliability might form a grouping. Again, consider what a grouping might indicate, and put it into words.
5. In the language of your customers, describe the outcomes they are trying to achieve.

Figure 3.2: Customer Outcomes

Tranquility	Power	Connection	Creativity	Security
Vitality	Service	Wisdom	Freedom	Strength
Beauty	Trust	Wonder	Exploration	Reliability
Wholeness	Energy	Entertainment	Convenience	Savings
Excellence	Faith	Education	Simplicity	Profit
Humor	Inclusiveness	Communication	Order	Gain

Your list of outcomes is a starting point. It provides insight into what your customers are trying to achieve, but it is not actionable yet. How can you purposefully deliver these outcomes to your clients?

1. For your top three outcomes, identify how your services deliver that outcome. What do your services do? How do they work? Why do they deliver these outcomes?
2. How could you amplify your services to really focus on these outcomes? What could you add, subtract, or enhance to create Function That Resonates?

Part 2: Authentic Differentiation

> There will always, one can assume, be the need for some selling. But the aim of marketing is to make selling superfluous. The aim of marketing is to know and understand the customer so well that the product or service fits him and sells itself.
>
> — *Peter Drucker, management guru*

Sticky Brands don't try to baffle or "sell" their clients into buying. Rather, they create compelling, authentic experiences that attract customers and bring them back again and again.

Differentiate your brand by giving customers an authentic experience at every opportunity. In this section you will learn how to:

- **Engage the Eye** by making your brand visibly different. Create a visual identity that makes your brand more attractive, more appealing, and visibly different.
- Create a **Total Customer Experience** by crafting a unique brand experience that brings your customers back again and again.
- Create interest in your brand by engaging your marketplace in conversations that get people to say, "**That's Interesting. Tell Me More.**"

Principle 4: Engage the Eye

Sticky Brands are visual brands. They engage their customers' eyes, because they know their customers judge them based on what they see. Sight is the most important human sense for evaluating brands and making purchase decisions.

Build a strong visual identity for your brand that engages your customers' eyes and lets them know your business is unique.

We Judge with Our Eyes

A picture is worth a thousand words, and your brand's visual identity is worth much more.

Your company's credibility is judged by its attractiveness. This is your visual identity, and it includes your logo, website, marketing material, and the imagery you use. It also radiates out to the design of your products and packaging, the appearance of your offices, and the way your people look.

Your brand will be judged at every visual touch point, and your customers will decide if your firm is a fit for them based on what they see. Is your company credible or not? Yes or no? Their eyes will make the decision.

We are visual beings, and the attractiveness of a person, a product, or a brand influences our attitudes. According to Dr. Richard Perloff, we are more likely to pay attention to an attractive person and remember what they say. Attraction cuts through the clutter, and we take note of it. Dr. Perloff writes, "Attractiveness becomes associated with the message. The pleasant affect one feels when gazing at a pretty woman or handsome guy gets merged with the message, resulting in an overall favorable evaluation of the topic."[11]

In the late seventies, Dr. Shelly Chaiken proved the power of attraction in an interesting study. She recruited a group of people of "high" and "low" physical appeal to test their persuasiveness. The group was instructed to approach students on a university campus and deliver a short pitch on why the school should stop serving meat in the cafeteria. They were effectively selling students on vegetarianism.

Each of the presenters delivered the same message. The only difference was the appearance of the speakers. The results varied widely between the attractive and unattractive speakers. The students who received the message from an attractive presenter were more inclined to agree that meat shouldn't be sold in the cafeteria than the students who heard it from the unattractive presenter.[12]

The impact of beauty travels beyond people. We are drawn to attractive products, buildings, and brands. Our eyes pull us toward things we find attractive. Attraction is magnetic. It is primal — it engages our lizard brains. We often assume beautiful things are better. For example, people assume Apple products are better because they have a high-quality finish and design. We also choose products and brands to enhance our own sense of self-worth. We may choose attractive things because it fits our notion of ourselves. Many people purchase luxury items to enhance their physical appeal.

The importance of creating an attractive brand has never been more important. We are glued to our smartphones, tablets, and computers. We get directed to websites and, in ten seconds or less, make a snap judgment based on its visual appeal. Does it have the information you need? If not, you're gone.

We are bombarded with visual stimuli. In our technology-driven society we rely on our sense of sight above all our other senses. Our senses of taste, touch, and smell do not play a major role in most of our purchases because we cannot rely on them. As a result, we naturally gravitate toward companies that deliver a better visual experience.

Sticky Brands pay a lot of attention to their visual identity and create optically engaging experiences for their customers.

Tell a Story with Your Images

Companies get lost in the evergreen forest by choosing safe, nondescript imagery for their brands.

For example, professional services firms like accountants, lawyers, and management consultants will often use imagery of their staff on their website and marketing materials. The shots are professionally taken and the images are attractive, but you could put those photos on any website. No one would be the wiser.

A decade ago those shots were cutting edge. The images firms used at the time were stock photography of puzzle pieces, stairs, compasses, and forests. They were metaphors for how the firm delivered value, but they became popular in the industry and quickly became cliché. The professionally shot staff photos were pretty nifty in 2005, but now they're cliché too.

Move beyond the visual clichés of your industry and tell a story. Your imagery is one of the first things a customer takes in, and it sets the stage to demonstrate what makes your business unique.

Beau's Brewery, a young company that's making waves in the craft brewing industry, has embraced its rural heritage to create a visual identity for its brand. In less than six years Beau's has grown from zero to over ten million dollars in revenue and now employs over seventy-five people. The company stands out as one of the most innovative brewers in North America. It's winning awards every season, and its beers are served in restaurants and pubs across the country.

All of this innovation and growth is originating from Vankleek Hill, a small rural town outside of Ottawa, Canada. Steve Beauchesne, co-founder and CEO of Beau's Brewery, likes to say, "The town has eighteen hundred people, two thousand cows, and one brewery." The picturesque town and the surrounding area are the inspiration for Beau's visual identity, and it sets the stage for how Beau's differentiates its brand from the goliaths of its industry.

Beau's owns its rural heritage and make it a central part of the business. Its tagline is "All Natural Brewing Company," and the theme radiates through its packaging, logo, website, and even its booths and displays. The company accentuates the theme by focusing on the imagery and experiences of small-town farming.

Steve Beauchesne explains, "My dad and I started Beau's in 2006, and the company started with five people in total. In one of our first major marketing initiatives we bought a booth at the Ottawa Wine and Food Show. We were close to dead broke at the time. We bought the space, but had nothing left over to buy a booth or invest in fancy marketing materials. We had to use what was around us."

Steve and his team built a booth out of hay bales and barnboard. "It cost us next to nothing, and it looked great," continues Steve. "The booth had an added bonus. It smelled incredible. The entire room picked up the great hay smell, and it drew people to us."

The Beau's team were keen observers and quickly noticed the rural theme resonated with their audience. People loved the experience and recognized Beau's as bringing back an experience of a more natural and simple time.

The team picked up a crucial insight and developed their visual identity around the theme of the small family farm. The family farm is a classic symbol for natural, wholesome, and pure products. The next time you are in the grocery store look at the product packaging in the dairy aisle. You will find images of an early twentieth-century farm with a barn, silo, and maybe a cow or two. These are images consumers associate with natural. Beau's has built its visual identity on a similar set of images. For example, the Beau's logo features a small tractor. (see Figure 4.1)

The brand imagery works brilliantly because it's built on a theme consumers already know. The belief is "the family farm is natural, and natural tastes better." Beau's builds off a heuristic consumers already believe, and that allows customers to quickly and easily understand its story.

To find the imagery for its packaging and visual identity, the Beau's team scoured their local landscape. They took pictures of

Figure 4.1:
The Beau's Brewery Tractor.

tractors, barns, and farming equipment. They looked for inspiration in the scenes they came across every day.

Beau's logo is an illustration of a fifties-style tractor. It's the kind of tractor that has two large rear wheels, a long engine cab in the front, and a riding seat on the back for the farmer to look up and over the fields. Jordan Bamworth, Beau's creative director and designer, developed the tractor logo. He explains, "The small tractor represents the idea of a family run business or a family farm, and it speaks to the agricultural quality of the Ottawa Valley and Vankleek Hill area."

The tractor logo was a bit controversial at first. Not everyone on the team was in agreement with using the tractor image. Tim Beauchesne, co-founder and Steve's father, wasn't convinced the tractor was the right image. He felt it conflicted with the company's commitment to "All Natural." He argued a tractor, especially a diesel tractor, spews out smoke and pollution. It's not natural compared to images of chicken, barley, and fields.

The Beau's team considered the criticism carefully, and evaluated competitors' visual identities. With a little analysis, it was evident that landscape and grain images are cliché in the craft-brewing industry. For example, Sierra Nevada Brewing Co.'s logo features a picturesque landscape of the Sierra Nevada foothills, and the picture is framed in barley and hops. Chicken images, especially ones of roosters, were rejected too, because a number of craft brewers already used them in their logos.

The small tractor was unique. The team decided that even though it burnt fossil fuels, it was small and quaint. "People don't perceive the small tractor as a gas guzzler like a Hummer or a massive John Deere combine," says Steve. It's an image from a time we associate with our grandparents, great-grandparents, and great-great-grandparents — depending which generation you fall into today.

The tractor image became the symbol for Beau's rural theme, and its story of the small family farm. Beau's draws on the farm theme in everything it does. The company's booths and displays continue to look like a farmer's market stall, with copious amounts of hay bales and barnboard.

Beau's packaging draws out the theme too. Its signature beer, Beau's Lug Tread, comes in a four-pack that is packaged in a faux wooden crate, seen in Figure 4.2. The corrugated box is designed to look like

Figure 4.2: Beau's Lug Tread beer. It is sold in a four pack that is packaged in a faux wooden crate and showcases Beau's commitment to its rural roots.

an old wooden milk crate with a handle in the center. The package is printed to look like wood, and the front has a picture of Beau's tractor logo with a scene of a family farm.

The product packaging creates a visual shorthand for Beau's theme: all natural. The experience brings the country to the city and creates an association of a company that is challenging conventions and approaching the beer industry from a unique angle.

Beau's has to challenge convention to stand out in the ultra-competitive beer industry. Anheuser-Busch is ranked as the twenty-second-largest advertiser in the United States, according to the AdAge Data Center. Its advertising budget was over $1.36 billion in 2011.[13] The craft brewing market is equally competitive. According to the Brewers Association, there were over 2,347 breweries operating in 2012, which sold an estimated 13,235,917 barrels of beer with an estimated value of $11.9 billion.[14]

It is startling to think how quickly Beau's Brewery is growing in such a competitive market, but that's what it is doing. It stands out like an orange tree in an evergreen forest by crafting remarkable beers and packaging them in a compelling visual identity.

The small tractor and unique, attractive packaging motivates first-time customers to try the beer. The identity then functions as a visual queue to encourage customers to seek Beau's out the next time they are buying beer.

Build Your Visual Identity Around a Metaphor

There are universal stories that span countries, cultures, languages, and dialects. The hero's journey, for example, is a story that comes up frequently in literature. Star Wars, Harry Potter, and Lord of the Rings are all modeled on this archetype. Even the ancient stories of Moses and Prometheus follow the structure.

The hero's journey is a story we are all comfortable with. The main character, the hero, is a normal everyday person who is tasked to complete an extraordinary quest. The journey stretches the hero's skills and capabilities, but he has the aid of his friends and mentors to assist him until he reaches the final task. The final task is the hero's burden, and he must complete it alone.

Archetypes like the hero's journey come up frequently in our stories and help shape our understanding of the world. At a base level these are deep metaphors — the building blocks of our archetypes and stories. Gerald Zaltman writes in *Marketing Metaphoria*, "Deep metaphors are enduring ways of perceiving things, making sense of what we encounter, and guiding our subsequent actions."[15]

Every great brand is built on a deep metaphor. Chevy trucks offer their customers "control," and that's reflected in their tagline, "Like a

Rock." The metaphor means Chevy trucks are reliable, secure, and tough. They offer the driver the control, through reliability and strength, to get a tough job done.

Coca-Cola's metaphor is "transformation." Coke transforms you, because it replenishes energy, hydrates, and refreshes. Coca-Cola brings out the idea of the transformation metaphor in campaigns like "Open Happiness" and "Twist the cap to refreshment." Coke is signaling to consumers that its brand delivers energy and vitality, which will transform your life for the better.

Zaltman's research was influential on me when I was developing LEAPJob's visual identity. We wanted to get beyond the clichés of our industry and work with a deep metaphor too. Recruiting is a professional service, and firms in our sector gravitate toward standard and predictable imagery: pictures of their staff; puzzle pieces to represent making the "right fit"; compasses to demonstrate guidance; or stock photography of beautiful, smiling people.

Zaltman writes in *How Customers Think*, "Marketers who wish to influence the stories that consumers create must build stories around archetypes, not stereotypes. A story built around an archetype involves a universal theme, that is, a core or deep metaphor simultaneously embedded in a unique setting."[16]

Zaltman found there are seven deep metaphors, which he calls the Seven Giants: balance (or imbalance), transformation, journey, container, connection, resource, and control. LEAPJob's deep metaphor is "journey."

I did a lot of research on career transitions and job-hunting and found a career is like a journey. We move toward destinations like retirement or a promotion. If someone is unhappy in his role, he might say "I'm stuck" or "I'm not getting the advancement I expected." People "change directions" or go down "new paths" with a new job. Some steps on a career journey come quickly, and others stop us dead in our tracks.

Careers are laden in the language of the journey metaphor. Once I identified this insight I dug deeper into the metaphor and tried to understand how LEAPJob aids people on their career journey. The phrase "leapfrog" kept coming up in our discussions. We'd say things like, "We don't just guide salespeople to find their next job, we help them leapfrog to the next stage in their career."

The words "leap" and "leapfrog" became the basis for our visual identity and helped us shape all aspects of our brand. The company name, LEAPJob, was a play on "leapfrog." The company's tagline was "LEAP for it." Our symbol was a leaping frog.

We commissioned an artist, Daren Crigler, to create a mascot and develop a series of illustrations for our visual identity. Daren created a mascot that was a bright green frog with red eyes, and a little tie and briefcase (see Figure 4.3). Internally we called him "Leapy the frog," because he was always in motion. We made sure he was always in the air, and never touching the ground.

Daren's illustrations are bright and fun and they have a sense of energy. One picture showed Leapy leapfrogging his briefcase. In another, Leapy is being shot from a cannon. The series took on a life of its own and we kept thinking of new ways we could make Leapy leap.

The combination of bright colors, fun scenes, and a leaping mascot created a powerful visual identity for LEAPJob. We didn't look like any other recruiting agency — we immediately stood out. Our website and marketing material told a visual story and the words supported it. That first visual impression went a long way to improve our website performance. It reduced the bounce rate, increased the time on-site, and increased the number of people who called.

Figure 4.3: LEAPJob developed a brand identity around Leapy the frog. The frog is always in motion, and builds on LEAPJob's deep metaphor: journey.

Deep metaphors make your brand stand out. Features and benefits have to be explained, but a strong visual identity tells the story and speaks to customers at an emotional level. This is the primary advantage of working with deep metaphors — they are universally understood. When your visual identity is anchored on a deep metaphor you don't have to explain what makes your business unique. Your customers can see it. They can experience it, and they gravitate toward the attractive images.

LEAPJob does not talk about its deep metaphor or explain why it's relevant. Rather, the customers experience it and it speaks to them. When job seekers call LEAPJob they will often say, "I'm ready to leap to my next job." The metaphor resonates with them and it creates a heightened sense of engagement and excitement that we couldn't achieve through our words or services.

Zaltman continues, "Marketers often focus on relatively inconsequential differences when segmenting markets and positioning products. Even though a difference may be statistically significant, it may be substantively inconsequential and unlikely to influence consumer behavior." Zaltman is pointing out a natural trap in marketing. We can get too close to our products and services and end up focusing on the minor differences that separate us from the competition. The little things that may seem relevant can lack the human connection to influence your customers' beliefs. This is the trap that leads companies to work with cliché images versus developing a visual identity based on a metaphor.

Deep metaphors transition you from cliché images to ones that tell a story and clearly differentiate your brand from the competition. The challenge is to move beyond the nuts and bolts of your business and consider which of the Seven Giant metaphors best represent your visual identity.

Manage Your Brand's First Impression

A strong visual identity creates a compelling first impression. It sets the stage for your brand, and signals to the customer the kind of experience your company will deliver.

To get the customer experience off on the right foot, focus on your deep metaphor and the story you want to wrap around it. Beau's deep metaphor is transformation — it guides people back to a simpler, more natural time. LEAPJob's metaphor is journey — it encourages people to leap for their next career. What is your deep metaphor and story?

Your visual identity has several elements: your logo; the imagery used in your marketing materials and website; icons and symbols; colors; fonts; and the overall layout of your materials. All of these components come together to tell your brand's visual story, but they also have to be focused. Compelling first impressions are pure and uncluttered. They convey meaning right away. Strip away all the extraneous images and noise that do not support or enhance your deep metaphor and story. The extra stuff can cause confusion. Your goal is to deliver one set of images that your target market intuitively understands.

Don't leave the experience to chance. Test your visual identity to see if the story is coming through clearly and creating positive first impressions. Survey a few people from outside your industry and ask them to examine your marketing materials. Ask them to explain what they see. Ask them if the images are telling them a story. Ask them what they feel. Pay close attention to their words. They will let you know if you have a strong visual identity that builds a positive first impression for your brand.

A Visual Identity Has a Shelf Life

Visual identities age and mature, and if they are not maintained they fall apart.

Your website is a very visible part of your brand's visual identity. It is easy for others to see when it's out of date, and the longer it's left unchecked the more harm it creates for your business and brand. Corporate websites tend to need a visual overhaul every two to four years. In the third year they start to look tired, and by the fourth they are looking dilapidated. An old, dated website is not attractive. It doesn't draw in your customers or demonstrate your company is a credible option. It demonstrates a company that lets things slide.

Visual identities need a tune up every twelve to thirty-six months, depending on your industry. For example, youth- and technology-focused companies have to update their visual identities much more frequently than companies in the manufacturing or construction sectors do. Regardless of the pace of your industry's change, it is important to recognize your visual identity requires frequent maintenance to remain relevant.

Your visual identity is influenced by two forces: fashion and innovation. First, fashions and tastes change. What looks hot today will look passé in a couple of years. Even established brands like Coca-Cola and Pepsi go through regular updates. Every time these brands launch a new campaign they update their visual identity to make sure it is connecting with their target market and telling their story from a fresh, new perspective. The big brands even update the core aspects of their visual identity on a regular basis. Both Coca-Cola and Pepsi have adjusted their logos over the past decade. These adjustments help keep their brands relevant for the times.

The second reason for updating your visual identity is innovation. You change your visual identity to reflect changes in your business and business model. As your business model evolves, you update your visual identity to ensure it is telling the right story, creating the right customer experiences, and delivering the right value proposition.

Many companies get caught in major updates to their visual identities because they do not keep pace with fashion and innovation. They might get into a new website project every four years, only to find it turns into an out-of-control home renovation. You thought you were buying a new website, and next thing you know your firm is into a complete rebranding, of its visual identity, with a new logo, letterhead, business cards, signage, and sales materials.

Massive rebrands are usually a sign of neglect. You can manage your visual identity on an ongoing basis, and make changes every year to keep your brand fresh and relevant. The goal is to engage your customers' eyes and demonstrate a more attractive option. This requires an ongoing investment. Set aside the budget and time to make improvements to your visual identity annually.

A Visual Brand Is a Sticky Brand

Sticky Brands take pride in the way they look. They sweat the little details, and deliver compelling visual experiences that Engage the Eye.

Make your business stand out by really working to enhance the visual appeal of your brand. Look to each customer touch point — website, marketing materials, your products, your office, and any other areas your customers engage with regularly — and consider how you can deliver a compelling visual experience.

It just makes good business sense to create a strong visual brand. The way you present your products and services influences your customers. But it's more than that. Focus on design, because you are passionate about your business, passionate about the work you are doing, and passionate about serving your customers. Demonstrate your passion for your business by putting your best foot forward every single time.

Exercise: Engage the Eye

Objective:

Create a visual experience using metaphors, stories, and imagery in order to make your brand visibly different.

Your Brand's Metaphor

To discover your brand's deep metaphor ask a few of your customers, suppliers, and staff to work through the steps below.

1. **Pick a story:** Have each participant pick a story about the company that resonates with them. It could be about how they first found your company, and how they felt about the experience. It could be a story about working with a member of your team. It could be a story about how they use your products and services, and the impact the products had on their day-to-day lives. Let them pick. Ask them to tell a meaningful story about their experience working with your company.

2. **Select pictures:** Instead of simply having the participants tell you a story, have them tell it with pictures. Think of this as a slideshow. Ask them to find five to twenty images to tell their story. Ask them to either print the pictures, or arrange them in a slide deck. The pictures are the key to this exercise, because it helps the storyteller to be more descriptive about their experience.

3. **Share the story:** Find a space where each participant can share their story. Give them at least fifteen minutes and ask them to be as thorough as possible. Have fun with the process. Let them share an epic tale. Also ask them to explain why they chose the pictures and what each one represents.

4. **Listen:** As the participants are sharing their story, listen for details and take notes. Write down the words and phrases they use. Document their story as it unfolds. Try not to judge or fill in any other details. Just listen, observe, and be very present.

5. **Find common phrases:** After the participant has completed their story review your notes. Look for common phrases, metaphors, or descriptions they used. Circle all of them.

6. **Identify the deep metaphors:** Go through your notes to see what phrases or metaphors came up the most frequently. Beside the commonly used phrases, try to associate a deep metaphor with each one: balance (or imbalance), transformation, journey, container, connection, resource, control.

7. **Pick your metaphors:** Which deep metaphors fit your brand? If you find multiple metaphors come up in the stories, prioritize the top two metaphors into a primary and secondary metaphor. These are your brand's deep metaphors.

By identifying your primary and secondary metaphors you can go deeper into the visual identity of your brand. You can get beyond clichés and stock photography to find images and stories that draw out the feelings and essence of your brand.

The final step is to build your deep metaphors into your marketing materials. Examine your website, logo, and related brand documents and identify a consistent way to visually present your deep metaphor. For example, at LEAPJob we used Leapy the frog to present our metaphor of journey. Leapy was always in motion.

How can you present your deep metaphors so your customers intuitively get it?

Principle 5: Total Customer Experience

Sticky Brands are built on a collection of experiences. It doesn't matter what the company promotes, it's what the customers experience that counts. The experience shapes the perception of the brand. Sticky Brands provide their customers compelling experiences that keep them coming back.

Find what makes your business unique and better, and bake that into the customer experience.

Less Talk, More Experience

You don't have to tell your customers why they should buy. Let them make up their own minds.

The idea of the unique selling proposition, or USP, has been around for over sixty years. It was a phrase coined by Rosser Reeves, the legendary advertising executive of the Ted Bates agency. Reeves believed the point of advertising is to sell. The USP was his strategy to identify a point of differentiation in a product and distill it down to a single phrase. For example, Reeves oversaw the development of the M&M's candy slogan, "Melts in your mouth, not in your hand." Reeves's unique selling proposition for M&M's gave consumers something to talk about and focused their experience. He told them what made the product remarkable, and used advertising to condition consumers to believe it.

The USP was an effective strategy in a kinder, simpler time. After a century of advertising, customers have been conditioned to question ads and salespeople. They are smarter, more cynical, and better edu-cated than ever before, and it's hard for them to take a company at its word. And why should they? The bulk of corporate communications are one-sided. All companies are trying to do is to sell their stuff.

Yes, it is still possible to use the old approach. A USP like "Melts in your mouth, not in your hand" can work today, but it will take millions, if not billions, of advertising dollars to condition those beliefs in con-sumers. As a result, leading companies are changing how they market and advertise. Where is the unique selling proposition for Virgin, Apple, or Starbucks? You don't see Apple stating, "We design game-changing, easy to use, and aesthetically pleasing consumer electronics." Rather you experience the claim.

The Apple Store is a remarkable concept when you compare it to tradi-tional electronics retailers. You can touch everything without feeling guilty and the staff is deeply passionate about the products. Apple has created an environment that invites consumers to experience its products on their own terms. You can play a game on an iPad, browse the web on an iMac, or check out Apple's latest gadget. Apple lets you try out products, and if you have a question, one of the Apple Associates is happy to assist you.

Consumers love the Apple Stores. There are always lineups of peo-ple tinkering with the products, and what is even more remarkable is that these people are proactively spending money. They aren't being sold, they're buying. Why? Apple understands its value proposition speaks for itself. Apple doesn't have to sell because the experience does it for them.

The Apple Store is an integral part of the brand experience. Tim Cook, Apple's CEO[17] said, "[Apple Stores] are the face of Apple for almost all of our customers.... People don't think about the Cupertino headquarters; they think about the local Apple Store." The model is making money. According to *RetailSails*, in 2012 the Apple Stores earned approximately $6,050 per square foot of store space. That's more than double Tiffany & Co.'s revenue per square foot of $3,017.[18]

Starbucks and Virgin take a similar approach. Every touch point of their brand works to create a compelling customer experience. Each touch point builds on the next, allowing their customers to build mean-ingful relationships with the brand by interacting with it.

This approach to marketing and developing customer experiences is a new development for the big brands. Prior to 2000 consumer brands invested heavily in advertising and push marketing to reach their target markets. Business-to-business companies, on the other hand, invested in hiring massive sales forces to engage their prospects and customers face to face and over the phone.

The strategy was push, push, push, and talk, talk, talk. But when every brand is clamoring for attention, it turns into white noise. Customers tune out the marketing and advertising and focus on the few companies that will serve their needs with a relevant experience. They choose companies, products, and services that naturally stand out from the crowd and offer real value.

This is your opportunity too. You do not need a massive budget or lots of resources to create compelling customer experiences. They can be created by purposefully serving your clients and working to delight them.

An Experience Shapes the Product

Apple, Virgin, and Starbucks are big companies with big budgets. Small- and mid-sized companies definitely don't have the resources to challenge the status quo by creating their own Apple Stores, nor do they have the ability to create a national advertising campaign like "Melts in your mouth, not in your hand." And that's not the point. Sticky Brands craft compelling customer experiences — experiences that engage and delight their customers.

For example, Purdys Chocolatier engages all its customers' senses with its chocolates and brand experience. Purdys Chocolatier is a manufacturer and retailer of premium chocolates. It operates over sixty retail locations, and has an online store with a global reach.

You will find a broad range of treats at a Purdys store. There's a counter of assorted chocolates, with delectable treats like Himalayan Pink Salt Caramels, all sorts of chocolate-covered nuts, truffles with your favorite liquors, Peanut Butter Daisies, and so much more. You can also get pre-packaged gift boxes, signature dark chocolates bars, ice cream cones, and on and on we can go. The store is a chocolate lover's paradise.

Purdys Chocolatier isn't simply selling sugary treats. You can buy chocolates anywhere — they are a commodity. Purdys stands out by creating a personal connection with their customers. Every touch point of its brand comes together to heighten the buying experience and elevate the meaning of the chocolates in the customers' minds.

Purdys carefully manages the customer experience. You can't purchase its treats at another retailer because Purdys doesn't wholesale its chocolates. You can only buy a Purdys treat from a Purdys store or the Purdys website. This level of control helps the company manage its clients' relationship with the chocolates and the brand and create compelling customer experiences.

Retail provides Purdys a direct connection to its clients. The chocolates engage your sense of taste and smell, but the retail experience works to engage your heart and mind. Karen Flavelle, CEO of Purdys Chocolatier explains, "You can't tell a client what to do with the chocolates, but you can ask them where the box of chocolates is going."

A simple question like that can shift the client's relationship with the brand. "The Purdys experience is anchored on two themes, memories and favorites," continues Karen. The Purdys sales associates like to ask their clients, "What is your favorite?" or "Where is the box of chocolates going?" They are simple, open-ended questions that engage the client. It gets them to pause for a moment, contemplate why they are buying a box of chocolates, and why the purchase is important for them.

Longtime Purdys clients all have favorites. Some are drawn to the Hedgehogs or Sweet Georgia Browns, some prefer the ice cream, and some have a favorite assorted chocolates. People tend to identify with a specific treat, and that becomes a lightning rod for the brand experience.

Memories are another powerful theme for the brand experience. According to Karen, people buy chocolates for special occasions: Christmas, New Years, Valentines, birthdays, and anniversaries. Asking for a story at the point of purchase shifts the buying experience from something a consumer has to do to something they are actively engaged in. "Where are the chocolates going?" is a question that gets the client to slow down and savor the moment.

I experienced this at the Purdys store in Toronto's Union Station, the busiest transit hub in Canada. It was Friday at 5:30 p.m., and the train station was packed. Commuters were bustling through the station. Some were waiting for the trains to arrive and others were running full tilt because they were late. It was a chaotic scene. Instead of waiting by the departure monitors, I decided to visit the Purdys store in the station. I had interviewed Karen the week before and I was curious to see her team in action.

I ordered a small assortment of chocolates, and partway through my order the sales associate, Nora, asked me if I had a favorite. I should have been expecting the question, but it caught me off guard in the hustle and bustle of the rush hour crush. I was surprised that a retail associate would spark a conversation in such a busy environment.

I told Nora I'm partial to Sweet Georgia Browns, but I love dark chocolate in general. She took a genuine interest and asked if I had tried their dark chocolate bars yet. I hadn't. She offered me a sample of two dark chocolates, one from Peru and one from Ecuador. The Peruvian was bright and fruity, and I thought it tasted a bit like cherries. The Ecuadorian was rich and smooth, and had a coffee note to it. Nora's question of preference led to an experience.

Again, Nora asked which one I preferred. I said I liked the brightness of the Peruvian and she shared that their customers are almost split in preference. She turned to the other associates behind the counter and asked which they preferred. Turns out all the Purdys associates at the Union Station store were partial to the Ecuadorian.

The question of favorites was powerful. I may have been in the store to "test the brand," but I walked away with a story. I learned a little bit about where chocolate comes from and how the *terroir* of a region affects the flavor. I also learned how people are drawn to different flavor profiles. It was a neat experience.

I ended up buying a lot more than I expected. In addition to my assorted box of chocolates, I picked out a few bars of the Peruvian and Ecuadorian to bring home for my family. I wanted to share the experience I had in the Purdys store and see which flavors they preferred.

My in-store experience on its own may seem a little mundane — any retailer can ask these questions. But the fact is, most don't. Creating a compelling customer experience is not rocket science. It takes self-awareness on the part of the front-line staff and direction from the company's leadership on how to engage customers. It's a question of focus and priorities.

Purdys stands out from other retailers by being purposeful in the brand experience. The company and its staff are very aware of the two themes: memories and favorites. The front-line staff is given ample room and time to interact with the customers and have conversations, as opposed to worrying about their sales-per-hour. Purdys invests deeply in its hiring and training practices to create a consistent in-store experience across its sixty-seven locations.

There's also a less quantifiable aspect of the Purdys experience. What made my experience so compelling was the curiosity Nora demonstrated. Authentic curiosity is an anomaly. Consumers aren't used to a sales associate taking a moment in a busy environment to ask a personal question and have a conversation. The simple act of engaging your customers with a question and being genuinely interested in their response creates a Sticky Brand experience.

Purdys' customers come back again and again because of the unique experience. The company's stores are an orange tree in the evergreen forest of the confectionary industry. Or, more aptly, a purple tree in an evergreen forest. Purdys uses copious amounts of purple in its stores, packaging, identity, and marketing. As Karen says, "When people in Vancouver see purple, they think Purdys." Purple is part of the company's visual identity, and that signals the treats and brand experience you are in for when you visit its stores.

But back to the experience. The chocolates are packed with meaning brought on by memories and favorites. Purdys conditions its clients to seek them out for a unique treat they couldn't get anywhere else. "Purdys' chocolates get packed with meaning. Some of our customers share stories of how their grandmothers always had a box of Purdys when they came to visit. The memory of eating a Hedgehog or a Sweet Georgia Brown are linked to memories of spending time with their grandmothers," continues Karen. "We hear lots of stories of how our customers use the chocolates. Some people give a box of chocolates for an anniversary gift and hide diamonds in the box. Others have the chocolates as part of a family tradition."

Asking a customer to share their story elevates your brand in their mind. It cuts through the clutter and creates an experience you cannot achieve with push marketing and advertising. Questions encourage your customers to share and participate in the buying experience, and take a little pride in their purchase.

We Are Hardwired to Spot Differences

Purdys' approach Authentically Differentiates its brand because the experience is unexpected. Consumers are so used to being herded through mass retailers that a simple question creates a memorable experience, and one people want to repeat.

We are hardwired to notice these differences. Try a little experiment. Go to your local mall and people watch. Find a bench or a comfortable spot where you can watch the action for a while. For the first few minutes, just enjoy the experience. Get into the groove and have some fun watching people pass you by. Once you are relaxed, start taking note of what catches your attention.

You won't notice most of the people, but every now and then something will catch your eye. A commotion amongst a group of people. A woman fumbling with her coat. A bright bag. An attractive person. Little differences can capture your attention.

The ability to notice differences is drawn from our "primitive" or "lizard brains." The lizard brain sits at the top of your spine and is the command center for your body. It controls your breathing, heart rate, muscles, and nervous system, and it can override your "thinking brain" when you are feeling threatened. For example, when you're frightened and jump, that is your lizard brain telling your muscles to pull back.

When you are people watching, it's your lizard brain taking in the stimuli and directing you to the interesting sights and scenes. It captures colors, movement, sounds, and other stimuli that separate an object from the landscape.

Your lizard brain is also influencing your emotions, such as feeling excited, nervous, threatened, happy, or confident. It governs your gut reactions. When you say something "feels right," that's your lizard brain at work. It is helping you make decisions below the surface of your thinking brain. Your lizard brain is at work all the time, observing and influencing your decisions.

Purdys caters to the lizard brain by creating an experience. The company's use of purple helps it stand out and catch customers' eyes, and the experience anchored by memories and favorites builds trust and preference. The brand engages people at a deep emotional level.

Here's the challenge for your brand. Does it engage your customers' lizard brains?

Take a moment to study your business and the varying points your prospects and customers interact with your company, your products and services, and your people:

1. Can you spot what makes your firm unique from the outside looking in?
2. Does each touch point work together to create a cohesive experience?
3. What kind of experience are you delivering: comfort, security, delight, inspiration, knowledge, guidance, humor, excitement?
4. Can people form a gut reaction about your firm?

Be critical. Do you look and act like everyone else in your industry, or do you stand out with an experience that speaks to the lizard brain?

Create a Total Customer Experience

If you travel through Central and Western Canada in the warmer months you will see orange pop-up tents in parking lots. The residents in the area make a clear association with the tents, "That's where I get my car windshield repaired."

DECO Windshield Repair is an auto-glass repair company, and they make repairing a windshield insanely easy. DECO sets up mobile repair centers under bright orange tents in parking lots of major grocery stores and shopping centers. The goal is to be where the customers are.

While DECO's customers are doing their errands, the DECO technicians will repair a windshield crack or chip. They don't replace windshields or do any major repairs. The technicians just fix cracks and chips "up to the size of a Toonie." For non-Canadians, a Toonie is a two-dollar coin that is just over an inch in diameter.

Orange is an important aspect of DECO's visual identity because it makes the company's repair kiosks highly visible in busy parking lots. The color engages customers' lizard brains. Matt Horne, CEO of DECO, explains, "Orange is the first color you pick up in peripheral vision. You'll catch it out of the corner of your eye."

Orange is a very robust color. It draws people in. "Orange is a comforting color up close. The color radiates warmth and happiness, because it combines the energy and stimulation of red with the cheerfulness of yellow," continues Matt.

While DECO's orange tents act as a beacon, the in-person experience solidifies the brand experience and brings people back again and again.

DECO Windshield Repair is a seasonal business. Every summer its employee ranks swell as the company brings on hundreds of university and college kids to staff the kiosks. DECO goes out of its way to hire bright, energetic students, and provide them with oodles of training to deliver the optimal client experience. Matt and his team have a clear goal for their employees, "We want DECO to be an asset on a resume."

The team is DECO's secret weapon. You are guaranteed to have a unique and pleasant experience when you visit a DECO kiosk. You will get your windshield repaired quickly and painlessly, and you'll interact with technicians who know what they're doing and are fun and engaging. Matt continues, "We take the time to educate our clients on what we're doing, and how to maintain the longevity of their windshield." It's that positive and interactive experience that Authentically Differentiates DECO and creates a Sticky Brand.

From the very start DECO has been challenging the status quo and proving to its industry that customers want better service. When DECO launched in 2006 they faced a lot of industry resistance. Competitors dismissed the company and its approach to car maintenance. The auto-glass repair industry traditionally operates from garages in industrial parks. They try to position themselves as mechanics and their facilities are designed to create an air of credibility. The competitors want to be perceived as "real mechanics" offering "expert service." DECO's approach was counter to the industry practices, and they were mocked for delivering auto repairs in parking lots.

The competition underestimated DECO's model and its ability to attract and engage customers. In 2012 DECO repaired over two hundred thousand windshields. That's a lot of fixed cracks and chips. Matt continues, "The Albertan auto-glass repair industry has experienced declining revenues of 15 percent year-over-year since 2009. At first the declines were blamed on the recession. The industry assumed people were waiting longer to fix their windshields, or were simply tolerating the chips and cracks. Five years later it's clear the recession is not the primary reason the traditional auto-glass repair companies are suffering." DECO bucked all these trends and grew by over 800 percent in the same period.[19]

DECO's unique customer experience is driving its growth. It has grown to over 150 employees, and it has been featured in multiple magazines and lists as one of Canada's fastest growing companies.

DECO maintains its brand experience through every customer touch point. You will see orange accented with black on the company's kiosks, trucks, uniforms, website, and mobile apps. They make sure you associate those colors with the DECO experience.

The other key dimension of the DECO experience is ease. You can get your windshield repaired in fifteen to twenty minutes, and you can do that while you run your errands. That ease carries through to the company's digital properties too. The website is easy to navigate and guides you to the nearest kiosk. Download the mobile app, and you can find the closest location, its hours of operation, directions, and even the price.

There is nothing new about windshield repair. The service has been around for decades, and there are well established brands in the industry. DECO Windshield Repair is challenging the status quo and creating a compelling customer experience, and that's driving its growth. Every touch point comes together to make a mundane service convenient and engaging.

The Experience Sells

Unique brand experiences engage your customers' lizard brains. It gets them to shift from comparing your products and services to the competition to choosing you first. The experience elevates your products and services above the herd.

Each place your customers engage with your brand is an opportunity to create a compelling experience. Look at all your customer touch points: website, apps, your facilities, salespeople, customer service, your products, marketing material, and any other place your customer may come in contact with your brand. Each of these points is an opportunity to engage your customers and enhance their experience.

There are two things that lead to making every touch point sell:

1. A clear point of differentiation.
2. A compelling experience around that point of differentiation.

A point of differentiation is that one thing that makes your brand stand out. Chances are it will draw from your Function That Resonates, but it could also be your customer service, approach to design, product innovation, unique in-store experience, or something else. It's that point in your brand that people recognize and identify as you.

Apple has a clear point of differentiation in design. Apple is often described as a "design company that happens to make consumer electronics." Customers can see Apple's focus on design in the products, the user interface of the devices, the store layouts, and advertising. They all radiate ease of use and a modern and clean feel.

Purdys Chocolatier's point of differentiation is their retail experience. You can buy chocolates and sweets virtually anywhere, but Purdys' treats are packed with meaning. The in-store experience heightens their clients' relationship with "favorites and memories" and creates a compelling reason to seek out their chocolates above and beyond the vast array of available options.

DECO Windshield Repair's point of differentiation is based on Function That Resonates: get your windshield repaired while shopping for groceries. The experience is heightened with a brand based on colors, a unique staffing model, and a fun and engaging client experience.

What is your company's point of differentiation? It will be drawn out of your core skills and assets. What does your company do better than anyone else? What aspects of your business resonate with your market? As you identify your point of differentiation, look for opportunities to distill it into a unique experience that your customers will identify with and which will bring them back again and again.

Exercise: Total Customer Experience

Objective:

Create memorable moments that will shape your customers' experience and expectations of your brand.

Primary Touch Points

Where do your customers connect the most with your brand? For Purdys it's at the retail locations, and DECO it's the kiosks. What are your primary customer touch points?

Look beyond the obvious, and consider how your customers interact with your:

- Website or mobile apps
- Retail location
- Phone service (inside sales or customer service)
- Partners (resellers, retailers, distributors, integrators, installers)
- Other customers
- Social media (Twitter, Facebook, LinkedIn, Instagram, and any other platforms on which your brand is active)
- The Internet (Google, Bing, review sites)

At each touch point ask a pointed question: "How can we improve the customer experience to delight our customers?"

Engage the Lizard Brain

We are naturally attuned to spot differences in our environment. How does your brand stand out?

Compare your brand's experience with your direct competitors. Do you deliver a unique experience? Is it compelling? If not, what do you have to change to make the purchase experience unique? Be critical. Focus on each of the customer touch points and identify how you can make them into a key aspect of your customers' experience.

Principle 6: "That's Interesting. Tell Me More."

The five best words you can hear a customer say are, "That's interesting. Tell me more." If you can get them to say that, you have caught their attention and they will listen to what you have to say. Sticky Brands cut through the clutter of their market and engage their customers with Brand Storylines — stories that engage them in a conversation and build relationships.

Overcome Customer Indifference

One of the greatest obstacles to sales is indifference.

Even though we live in a world of immense choice, customers will primarily choose what they already know. It's not that they reject one option for another. Rather, they select options they are already comfortable with. Once a customer finds a brand that satisfies them, they usually don't experiment with new ones. All customers, both business and consumer, demonstrate brand loyalty.

Buying is habitual; it plays to our lizard brains. As we discussed in Principle 1: Simple Clarity, people will generally avoid deep thinking and contemplation on a topic. Why invest a lot of time researching options for common purchases? It's easier to choose what you already know.

You may be passionate about your business and its capabilities, but that doesn't mean anyone else cares. The majority of potential customers you will come across are perfectly content. They are making decisions and solving problems on a daily basis. They have their preferred suppliers and they know how to get things done. From their point of view, "If it ain't broke, don't fix it." That buyer indifference can be infuriating. It's one thing to have a customer reject you, that's manageable. You can learn from the experience and get better. Being ignored is entirely different, because your prospects are on autopilot and choosing the status quo.

Sticky Brands don't take indifference lightly. The goal is to stand out and capture your customers' attention. You won't stand out by being incrementally better than the big guys. You have to give your prospects, customers, and partners a reason to pay attention.

An effective way to engage your entire market is to engage people in a conversation. Instead of marketing to them, speak with them. Share ideas. Find common ground. Have a conversation and engage as much of your market as possible in topics that will motivate them to say, "That's interesting. Tell me more."

Conversations start with you. How can you spark a discussion? How can you get your customers to engage with you even if they're not buying right now?

Stand Out with Brand Storylines

Brand Storylines are a tool for sparking conversation — conversations that build relationships, demonstrate your firm's expertise, and generate top-of-mind awareness.

A conversation is a powerful way of ripping your brand out of the trap of indifference. It's easy to ignore companies that don't engage you, but it's hard to ignore a conversation. A conversation is a two-way dialogue to share ideas and opinions. It gets thinking started and it fosters personal connections. That spark of engagement can shatter the indifference trap, creating an opportunity for your brand to stand out and give your market a reason to try something new.

Not all conversations are equal. Brand Storylines are crafted to make your brand sticky. Brand Storylines have three key elements:

1. Expertise: It's a topic you know well, and draws from your company's core skills and assets.
2. Strong Opinions: It's a topic you are passionate about, and can take a stance on.
3. Point of Sharing: The topic resonates with your market, and encourages others to participate.

The three elements function as a three-legged stool. If any one of them is missing, the Brand Storyline is unsustainable. Strong Opinions without Expertise is a rant. Expertise without a Strong Opinion is boring, and without a Point of Sharing you're talking to yourself.

Each element is essential for crafting Brand Storylines that get your brand out of the indifference trap.

Expertise: Brand Storylines Are Drawn from Strengths

Whenever you can engage someone with a story, you know you are on the right path.

Stories shift the customer experience and plant the seed of a relationship. A story opens things up because it's the start of a conversation. You can share ideas and engage your market in a dialogue.

Muldoon's Coffee engages its entire market with two Brand Storylines: "Why go out for coffee?" and "The Green Office."

Muldoon's Coffee is a corporate coffee service, and it has a simple but ambitious goal. Shaun Muldoon, CEO of Muldoon's, explains, "Our mission is to give employees a reason to stay in the office for coffee. In the early 2000s we saw the growth of Starbucks and other specialty coffee houses as a signal of what professionals want. They want a great cup of coffee, and they will go out of their way to get it. Our goal is to offer the taste and experience they expect, but make it far more accessible."

Muldoon's Coffee operates in the highly competitive corporate coffee market. It competes with giant food services companies, but stands out with a superior product and service. The core of its Authentic Differentiation is Function That Resonates: better tasting coffee in your office. Muldoon's achieves Function That Resonates with core skills and assets that separate them from the vast array of coffee services available to companies.

First, they are a roastery. Muldoon's roasts its own beans to ensure flavor, freshness, and quality. Second, its single-serve brewing system not only delivers a convenient, great tasting cup of coffee, it is environmentally friendly. Third, it has a service model that is uniquely its own. Muldoon's approaches customer service with a zeal that is unusual in its sector.

Muldoon's stands out on its core skills and assets alone, but the company is driven to grow. The company's revenue has more than doubled in the past five years, and it is growing by 23 percent year-over-year. To maintain this pace of growth, Muldoon's is constantly working to grow its brand awareness. To this end, Muldoon's draws from its core skills and assets to craft its two Brand Storylines.

The first storyline, "Why go out for coffee," is based on the taste of the coffee. Most of Muldoon's customers prefer the taste of Muldoon's to other options. Instead of bragging about how good its coffee tastes — which is very subjective — Muldoon's talks about the "corporate productivity drain" of employees going out for coffee. Shaun explains, "An average employee spends over 125 hours a year going out for coffee. That's 6 percent of the employee's salary, or three weeks of vacation." That's a startling statistic. He continues, "Professionals, especially young professionals, want a good cup of coffee. They are not going to drink the stale vending machine stuff in their office. They're going to get a good coffee."

Shaun's numbers are conservative. It's a basic calculation that employees go out for coffee half an hour per day over fifty weeks. In a downtown office tower there is no way you can do a coffee run in under thirty minutes, especially when you look at the lines at Starbucks and other premium coffee shops.

The impact on lost productivity catches business owners' and chief financial officers' attention right away. Just do the math. The payroll of a small software firm with seventy-five employees is roughly $6.4 million. If 60 percent of its staff are coffee addicts and go to Starbucks daily, it's costing the firm over $230,400 in lost productivity annually.

With some research and a bit of spin, Muldoon's has shifted a key feature — taste — into a Brand Storyline about corporate productivity. By simply stating "6 percent of your payroll is walking out the door for coffee," Muldoon's engages its market in a conversation.

It's not hard for Muldoon's to stoke the flames of a conversation on this storyline. A lot of employees dislike the taste of office coffee. "The reason most office coffee doesn't taste very good is the coffee is stale. Even mainstream single-serve brewing systems are packaged with coffee that has been purposefully staled so it can be contained in a hard plastic container," says Shaun.

Freshly roasted coffee beans release carbon dioxide and other gases. This is part of their flavor profile. A fresh cup of coffee tastes amazing, because it engages both your sense of taste and smell. The challenge is those coffee gases are difficult to package, especially for most single-serve brewing systems. "If the hard container packs were filled with fresh coffee the packages would burst," says Shaun. "The package is vacuum sealed in hard containers, and there's no way to vent the gases being released from the beans. Manufacturers prevent package damage by airing the freshly roasted coffee for a few days to de-gas or stale it before it's packaged." The result for consumers is a bland cup of coffee, and that creates an opportunity for Muldoon's to engage people in a conversation. The company can point out the traditional office coffee options don't taste very good, and professional employees will solve the problem by going out for the good stuff.

Figure 6.1: Muldoon's Singles are 100 percent biodegradable and deliver an exceptional cup of coffee.

"Why go out for coffee?" is a simple and portable Brand Storyline. It is an easy idea for others to grab onto, and it creates a water-cooler moment. People can lament about why they hate the coffee in their staff room, discuss how going out for Starbucks is becoming the new smoke break, or share ideas on how to improve employee morale and productivity. It's a versatile storyline that has traveled well beyond Muldoon's, but it comes back to the company because it is the originator of the research.

Muldoon's second Brand Storyline, the Green Office, also plays to their core skills and assets. "We created an environmentally friendly brewing system, because that's what our customers wanted," says Shaun. Muldoon's brewing system does not use hard plastic packaging like mainstream office coffee systems. The company uses pouches that look a little bit like an oversized and over-packed tea bag, as you can see in Figure 6.1. The Muldoon's Singles are 100 percent biodegradable and come in a minimalist film wrapper that's recyclable.

Muldoon's focus on creating a green product is another potent storyline. Sustainability and green initiatives are of keen interest to many companies, and the storyline travels both ways. On one side Muldoon's employees can talk about how their products are green, but on the other side they can share ideas on green manufacturing, distribution, and business systems.

By sharing information you can have a meaningful two-way conversation and get away from the peacocking of sales and marketing. It creates a give-and-take relationship. Muldoon's can share what it is doing and how it is innovating on the topic of sustainability, but it can also be inquisitive and learn from others. The nature of these conversations make Muldoon's far more meaningful and authentic, and that fosters deeper personal relationships.

Muldoon's combines the two storylines to engage its market in conversation. Some people are drawn to the taste stories while others are more engaged in the green topic. Both stories complement each other and build on the firm's strengths. The storylines come from an area of passion, and that makes the conversations more relevant, engaging, and fun.

The value of this level of engagement is sales. Conversations fill the top of Muldoon's sales funnel. They are the seeds of relationships that get people to think of Muldoon's first when they're considering options for their office.

Strong Opinions: Brand Storylines Start with Passion

Brand Storylines are manufactured. Muldoon's Coffee didn't just start talking about the "Green Office" or how "6 percent of your payroll is walking out the door for coffee." Muldoon's crafted these stories because they are connected to two clear strengths of the company.

The reason these stories are sticky and spark conversation is that Muldoon's is taking a stance. It is not sitting on the fence or giving a balanced argument. No, the company is sharing its opinion of how employees will behave when you give them vending machine–grade coffee. It is also taking the stance that keeping employees in the office is better than having them go out for their breaks.

Muldoon's stance is polarizing, and that's what makes the conversations interesting and engaging. Some people agree, while others do not. Both routes are excellent, because they engage people, encourage them to share ideas, and build relationships.

Any company of any size can engage its market in a conversation. One of the most famous Brand Storylines is the Dove Campaign for Real Beauty. Dove created a worldwide conversation about beauty, women in advertising, and women taking pride in who they are. The campaign broke down barriers and created a real conversation with Dove's customers, women, and the media at large.

For example, in 2013 Dove released a three-minute video titled *Real Beauty Sketches*. The film demonstrated how women perceive themselves and contrasted that view with how others see them. In the film, Gil Zamora, an FBI-trained forensic sketch artist, draws a picture of each woman based on her self-perception. The next day, Zamora creates another drawing of each woman based on the description of a stranger. The sketch artist and the participants cannot see each other, and Zamora is drawing them solely based on their verbal descriptions.[20] The film creates a stark contrast of how women perceive themselves and their flaws, and how others see them. The strangers' descriptions of the women were far more flattering, and the drawings were much more attractive and closer to what the participants actually looked like.

The video is effective because it hammers home Dove's Strong Opinion that all women are beautiful. Lois Kelly writes in *Beyond Buzz*, "Dove's campaign began with a point of view, based on consumer insights that beauty comes in all ages, shapes, and sizes. Beauty is not defined by youthfulness or slenderness or a flawless complexion. There is no image of beauty."[21]

The Campaign for Real Beauty takes a contrarian stance. Rather than portraying supermodels and beautiful celebrities to promote their products, Dove presents "normal" women and celebrates what makes them beautiful.

Real Beauty Sketches captured the essence of Dove's opinions of beauty, and the message resonated with its target market. According to *AdAge* the short video was one of the most watched ads of all time. Within ten days of being released the film was viewed over thirty million times on YouTube, and had over 660,000 Facebook shares.[22] "Dove's point of view hit a nerve," continues Kelly. "The point of view gives the campaign conversational value — whether you've seen the campaign or have simply heard about it. Points of view get attention and stir up talk."

Dove is a big brand with a big advertising budget, but its approach to sparking conversations with Strong Opinions is accessible to all companies. Conversations are not expensive. Anyone can have them. All it takes is taking a stance on an interesting and relevant idea.

The challenge — and the part that scares many companies away from working with Brand Storylines — is taking a stance. The fear is always, "What if we offend a potential customer?" Or, "What if they disagree with us?" That fear of resistance destroys effective marketing, and it strips away the potency and interest from a conversation. Balanced is boring, and boring doesn't travel.

Professional services firms are particularly guilty of watering down their opinions because they want to present their brands as big and credible. They want to create an air of professionalism, and sharing Strong Opinions could be perceived as chipping away some of the pristine veneer of the firm.

But that veneer is not doing the brand any favors. You don't create Authentic Differentiation by muting your personality or being like someone else. It doesn't help your company stand out. It doesn't make your people more interesting or accessible. It doesn't do anything to Tilt the Odds.

Rather the veneer makes your company look more like a knockoff of the big guys, and it keeps your brand firmly stuck in the soft, squishy middle.

Take a stance. Share your opinions. Let people know what your company believes.

When we developed LEAPJob's Brand Storylines we paid close attention to our Strong Opinions on core sales topics. In our content we continually kicked the hornets' nest with storylines like, "cold calling is dead," "salespeople don't drive growth, they serve it," and "salespeople leave weak brands." The ideas were polarizing in our target market. We were engaging both sales professionals and business leaders, and many of the topics struck a nerve.

The "cold calling is dead" series was by far our most popular. We came out with a clear stance that companies that relied on cold calling as their primary source of lead generation were not only failing themselves, they were failing their salespeople. We argued that cold calling was an old and dated means of marketing, and modern companies treated demand generation as a business function.

The storylines were bold and they triggered conversation. We always found a strong majority of people agreed, but the ones who disagreed with us were passionately vocal. They argued their points, and shared their opinions. The storylines triggered intellectual and engaging debates.

There were no right or wrong answers, because we were all sharing our opinions. It wasn't about education — it was about debate and conversation. And it was fun. The debates formed relationships and built brand awareness. People got to know us and our approach, and when they had a need they'd call us first.

Take a stance in your brand. What do you talk about with colleagues at cocktail parties or events? You may start with the weather, but that gets boring quickly. Where do you have the best conversations? What topics or ideas engage people? What do you talk about with people who aren't customers, and probably never will be either?

The business conversations that you gravitate toward are the seeds of your brand's opinions. They are the things you care about and believe in. You can catch yourself pushing toward your Strong Opinions when you use phrases like "I believe," "from my perspective," or "I think." These phrases will help you identify your brand's opinions.

People may not agree with your company's Strong Opinions, but they will not ignore them either. Your opinions make you more interesting as a person, and they also make your company more appealing as a brand. They Authentically Differentiate your company. Choose Brand Storylines where you can share your perspective on the topic and take a stance.

Point of Sharing: Connect the Brand Storyline to Your Market

A Brand Storyline that doesn't engage your market in a conversation is of little value. To break through the indifference trap you need to spark a two-way dialogue with your market. You are aiming for the phrase, "That's interesting. Tell me more."

The Point of Sharing is the connective glue of your Brand Storyline. It's the bond that engages the other party and propels them to have a conversation. The Point of Sharing is what makes the storyline sticky, and makes it resonate with your target market.

A Point of Sharing can be based on a shared interest, a shared experience, or a shared value. A shared interest is a topic or idea you have in common with your target market. Muldoon's Green Office storyline is based on a shared interest. The topic engages people who are interested in sustainability and greening the workplace, and it provides the connective glue for a conversation. Shared interests are the most common storylines in a business-to-business market. These conversations tend to be business oriented and appeal to a large audience.

Shared values are storylines that are personal and universal. The Dove Campaign for Real Beauty is based on a shared value. Dove leads with a clear value statement that "all women are beautiful." Shared values are broad topics and usually revolve around the environment, religion, equality, human rights, or preventing poverty. They are ideals people believe in and are passionate about. People not only love to talk about their values, they like to work with others to act on them too. A Brand Storyline organized on a shared value can be very powerful, but also very polarizing. Companies with value-driven brands lean toward storylines based on shared values.

Shared experiences come in many forms. They can be life-changing events like an accident or a divorce, or they can come from growing up as a minority in a certain culture. The experience brings together like-minded people, who form a bond around their shared experience. The best way to describe a shared experience is the phrase, "it takes two to know one." Some companies have gone through distinct situations or experiences such as a succession, merger, rebranding, or downsizing. That shared experience creates the seed of a conversation. Companies with a community focus will gravitate toward shared experience storylines.

Brand Storylines capitalize on a Point of Sharing to make the topic sticky. The goal is to find a topic your audience can proactively participate in. It gives them a reason to engage with you and share their opinions on the topic.

A Brand Storyline without a Point of Sharing is just marketing. You are preaching at your market and hoping they will respond. The Point of Sharing acknowledges you are choosing a topic that will resonate with your market and encouraging others to give back.

Crafting your Brand Storylines will draw from all three elements: Expertise, Strong Opinions, and a Point of Sharing. They take effort to craft, and involve testing to find the storylines that resonate.

Conversations Make Your Brand Sticky

Everyone has an opportunity to engage their market in a conversation. It's an added layer in your marketing and content communications. A company that only talks about itself and its products gets boring pretty quickly. You probably wouldn't want to follow a blog or subscribe to an email newsletter that was constantly pitching to you.

Brand Storylines are a powerful, sustainable, and cost-effective way to engage your customers. We have conversations every day. There is no reason why your brand can't engage your market in interesting and relevant conversations too.

The challenge is finding Brand Storylines that fit your company. The Dove Campaign for Real Beauty is effective because Dove is taking a contrarian stance in the cosmetics industry. Muldoon's catches your attention with a statement that professional employees will go out of their way to buy a good coffee. Each storyline is unique to the brand, and they just fit.

What conversations do you want to spark in your market?

Brand Storylines are organic, authentic, sustainable, and they build relationships. And that's so important. When you have a relationship, you can break free of the indifference trap and be your customers' first choice. Conversations make your brand sticky.

Exercise: "That's Interesting. Tell Me More."

Objective:

Develop one or two Brand Storylines to engage your market, spark conversations, and build relationships.

Take a Stance

Sticky Brands are not afraid to share their opinions. In fact, sharing Strong Opinions is what makes them stand out and attract like-minded customers to them. Identify some areas your brand takes a stance.

Try completing some of these statements:

- We believe …
- Our competitors get it wrong, because …
- What frustrates us about our industry is …
- What surprises most people about our approach is …
- We never want to be associated with …
- People commonly says this, but we think it's actually …
- What gets me most excited about our industry is …
- The biggest risk to our customers is …

Find strong statements where you can share your opinions and beliefs. Look at the topics your business speaks to, and give a real hardline stance on what they mean for you and your brand.

Part 3: Punch Outside Your Weight Class

If you don't blow your own horn, someone else will use it as a spittoon.

— *Ken Blanchard, author of fifty books, including* The One Minute Manager

Sticky Brands are savvy marketers. They blow their own horns, and make sure their business stands out in their marketplace. They use all the tools and tactics at their disposal to stand out, attract customers, and drive sales.

Make your brand so visible and engaging that it is hard to ignore. Be everywhere. Build relationships. Be your customers' first call.

In this section you will learn how to:

- Develop a **First Call Advantage** for your business by building relationships with your target market upwards of three years before they have a need for your services.
- Make your brand appear to **Be Everywhere** by building a community to engage your market and build relationships.
- **Pick Your Priorities** to drive sales and grow a Sticky Brand by focusing on one priority at a time: Volume, Velocity, or Value.

Principle 7: First Call Advantage

Sticky Brands are their customers' first call when they are ready to buy. It's a powerful sales position. A First Call Advantage sets customer expectations and provides an opportunity to solve their needs before they shop anywhere else.

Build relationships with your market — prospects, customers, and referral partners — upwards of three years before they need your services.

Build Your Brand Early and Often

The best time to initiate a client relationship is three years before your services are needed.

Sticky Brands build relationships early and often, because relationships are the difference between being your customers' first choice and fighting it out with your competition. When you connect and build relationships with your customers before they need you, they will seek you out when they are ready to buy.

It's a matter of trust. Your customers aren't going to buy from you unless they like your company and trust it. It's that simple. If they don't like you, they will look for alternatives. If they don't trust you, they will never buy. By seeding relationships early and often, Sticky Brands become appreciated and trusted before the buying process even begins. That means when a customer has a need they will call the company they know, like, and trust before anyone else.

Even consumer brands like Coca-Cola, Tide, and Heinz Ketchup establish strong relationships with their customers. They may not be personal connections, but those companies have established a relationship by delivering a consistent product for over fifty years. Consumers like what these brands deliver, and trust they will have a consistent experience. Even though these products are widely accessible and easy to buy, the relationships these brands form with customers are a differentiating factor. The relationship fosters brand loyalty and drives consumers to choose them over generic, low-cost options.

Being liked and trusted is the key building block of the buying process. Brand awareness is important, but it's irrelevant if your customers do not like you and trust you. People buy based on their relationship with the brand. And the more complex the product or service, the more important that relationship becomes. That's why three years is so important. Build relationships before they are needed. It makes all the difference in the world for your brand.

Sales Has Changed

Most marketing messages not only fail to build relationships, they fall on deaf ears. At any given time the vast majority of potential customers are not buying. Marketing focused on promoting and selling more products only speaks to a small segment of the market: active buyers who have a need and are shopping right now.

What about everyone else? What about future customers? What about the people who don't have a need today, but will someday? They are not paying attention to promotions and ads. They're not interested in a sales pitch — at least, not right now. Paul Emond, CEO of Versature, sums up the dilemma nicely, "When people aren't in the buying mode, they don't want to be sold to."

Versature is a business-phone service. They deliver Hosted-PBX and VoIP phone services to small- and medium-sized companies across Canada. Versature provides businesses advanced features like call recording, voicemail-to-email, and integration with *Salesforce.com* — features you wouldn't normally get from a traditional phone company. But if a customer isn't in the market for new phone services, all the features and benefits don't matter. They're not going to listen.

Versature discovered the hard way that traditional sales and marketing tactics are ineffective on prospects and customers that aren't buying right now. Paul explains, "We were founded in 2003, and for the first few years we had a traditional approach to sales. I had two full-time salespeople, and an outsourced appointment setting service. We ran direct marketing campaigns, and we called on the local businesses in our area."

On paper Versature had a culture of sales and the "right approach" to build relationships and acquire customers, but it wasn't achieving its goals. Paul continues, "We pushed and pushed, but we weren't getting the results we expected. When people aren't in the mode to replace their phone system they don't want to talk about it, or even think about it."

Versature was caught in the classic sales and marketing model that is prescribed to many small businesses. The assumption is that to drive sales you need good salespeople to knock on a lot of doors and do a lot of selling. That's the old model of selling, and it is broken.

The core methodologies and approach to professional selling originated in the mid-seventies from large companies like IBM and Xerox. The term "solution selling" was coined in 1975 by Frank Watts while he worked at Wang Laboratories. Programs like SPIN Selling, Strategic Selling, and Solution Selling all came from people working to evolve the selling methodologies at big companies. This made sense for the time. During the seventies, eighties, and nineties, companies invested heavily in the science of selling because salespeople were the most efficient and effective conduits for distributing complex product information. Companies hired massive sales forces to prospect, build relationships, distribute product information, and sell. And they coupled that hiring with training programs to deliver more predictable sales results.

The role of the sales force has changed. Small- and mid-sized companies don't need massive sales forces to distribute product information anymore. Advancements in the Internet, telecommunications, and mobile technologies provide companies far faster and easier ways to distribute and share product information and company news. More importantly, customers don't use salespeople to find information. They've got Google. If there is something they want to know, they can search for it.

We live in a world where information is readily available. The Internet makes it easy to distribute information, ideas, and connections. Customers are savvy, well-educated buyers, and in many cases they know as much about the products and services they are buying as the salespeople who are selling them. They're not waiting by the phone to have a conversation about your products and services when they don't have a need. They'll look your company up or find it when they are ready.

The traditional approach to sales and marketing is futile when used on a non-buying audience. It doesn't matter how good your products or services are. It doesn't matter how much money you can save your clients. It doesn't matter how much you think you can help a company. If the customer is not ready to buy, they're not going to listen.

The 3% Rule

The 3% Rule, featured in Figure 7.1 (facing page), is a model to segment your market into buying groups. The triangle represents your market, which is anyone who could buy your products and services: customers, past customers, and prospects.

The 3% Rule divides your market into two fundamental groups. The top 10 percent of the triangle are buyers. They have a need and they're willing to act on it. The lower 90 percent don't have a need for your services right now, and any sales or marketing pitch will fall on deaf ears. What this means is there are two modes of building relationships and creating demand for your products and services.

The Top 10 Percent

The Top 10 Percent of the model are sales leads.

Three percent are active buyers. The very top of the triangle are the active buyers. This is the segment of your market that has a need, they've made a commitment to change, and they are actively shopping for solutions.

Seven percent intend to change. This next segment has a need for your services, but they are not proactively looking for them yet. They're not

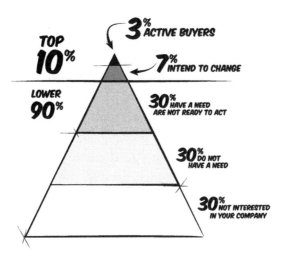

Figure 7.1: The 3% Rule.

searching Google for answers or requesting referrals. A well-timed cold call or marketing campaign can be very effective on this segment because you are delivering a solution before they start shopping.

Sticky Brands target the Top 10 Percent by placing their brand in the Path of Search. This is a defined window of opportunity when a prospect or client has a need. If you haven't already established a relationship with the customer, then your brand needs to be in the right place at the right time to be considered.

How do your customers look for your services when they have a need? Do they search Google, ask for a referral, or something else? Versature generates a significant number of sales leads every month from people searching Google for business phone systems. To capitalize on this behavior, Versature invests heavily in search marketing — search engine optimization, pay-per-click advertising, and digital marketing — to place their brand in the Path of Search. This investment more than pays for itself. Versature achieves a twelve-to-one return on every dollar they spend on Google.

Marketing to the Top 10 Percent focuses on making your brand stand out and be highly visible when a buyer has a need.

The Lower 90 Percent

The Lower 90 Percent of your market are not shopping right now.

Thirty percent have a need, but not enough to change. These buyers are just below the 10-percent line. They have a need or a problem you can solve, but they are not ready to act on it yet. They have other priorities. Until the need becomes more pressing, they won't enter the Top 10 Percent and be prepared to make a purchase.

This is a frustrating segment because salespeople often think these people are buyers in the Top 10 Percent. The salesperson can see the need and the buyer is receptive to having a conversation, but the sales cycle just keeps dragging on and on. The problem is the customer is not ready to buy, and trying to "close a deal" is futile.

Thirty percent are content, and definitely won't change. This segment of your market do not have a need. They may have recently purchased another solution. They may be too small for your services. They may not be experiencing any of the issues your services resolve. Either way, they're not buying and any sales or marketing message will fall on deaf ears with this segment.

Thirty percent are not interested in your company, period. The segment at the bottom of the triangle is a portion of your market who will not buy from your company. Basically, they will never choose you no matter how good your products are or how persuasive your salespeople are. These can be companies with loyalty to your competitors, past customers that had a bad experience, or companies that just aren't a good fit for you. Don't sweat it. Just recognize that there is a portion of your market you won't sell to — your brand can't be all things to all people.

The Lower 90 Percent of the 3% Rule is challenging, because these customers are not receptive to traditional marketing messages. They don't care about benefit statements, value propositions, product innovations, industry gossip, or why your company is great. But this is also your golden opportunity. Even though the Lower 90 Percent don't have a need for your services, it doesn't mean you can't build a relationship with them. If you build and scale relationships with the Lower 90 Percent they will call you first when they are ready to buy.

Brands Are Built in the Lower 90 Percent

Sticky Brands are built by engaging their market early and often. They focus on the Lower 90 Percent to build relationships and be their customers' first call when they are ready to buy.

Jim Gilbert's Wheels and Deals, who we discussed in Principle 2: Function That Resonates, builds relationships with small acts of generosity. The company keeps its brand top of mind with its customers year after year by acknowledging birthdays.

People are at their most reflective on New Year's Day and their birthday. These are milestone dates. Another year has passed and it causes people to reflect, ponder, and plan for the future. On birthdays and New Year's people consider what they achieved in the past year. Did they hit their goals? Are they happy? What resolutions should they make for the upcoming year? Our work life and personal life are linked. Our successes or failures at work directly impact our sense of self-worth and happiness. The same is true on the personal side. Problems at home can greatly impact work performance. I think it's next to impossible to separate these two worlds. They are tightly integrated. That is why birthdays and New Year's are such important dates. These are opportune times for marketers, and a timely message can be very impactful.

Wheels and Deals started their birthday program in 2000. The idea for the program came from Joe Girard, recognized as "the world's greatest salesman" by the *Guinness Book of World Records*. One of Girard's strategies was to send all of his customers a birthday card every year. The cards kept his name front and center, and customers called him first when they were in the market for a new vehicle.

Jim Gilbert took the idea and built on it. Wheels and Deals create a custom gift every year. They are little keepsakes that delight their customers. The program reached over twelve thousand people in 2013, and it helps reinforce the many relationships Wheels and Deals has developed over the years. The program resonates with the market because the simple acknowledgement demonstrates the company cares and it keeps the brand top of mind.

For example, Jim shared a letter he received from a customer:

Hi Jim,

A few years ago, my husband and I bought a beautiful yellow, 911 Porsche Carrera from you. We've had a lot of fun with it during the two summers we've had it and are anxiously waiting for the snow to melt (and the potholes to be repaired) to get it back on the road.

Yesterday, I got a dog leash in the mail from you — my second one, which is great because we have two dogs. Anyway, I am writing to thank you for that and for the other little surprises we've received from you from time to time. We've never had a used car buying experience quite like the one we had with your company. It was exceptional and the exceptional touches, like the leash, just keep coming.

I thought I'd write to say thank you. You can be assured that we recommend you to anyone we know who is buying a car.

Sincerely,
Ruth

Wheels and Deals invests over one hundred thousand dollars a year on the program, but the impact is remarkable. The gifts build relationships with the Lower 90 Percent.

Ruth doesn't have a need right now, but she is actively engaged with Wheels and Deals. When she enters the Top 10 Percent she will call Wheels and Deals first, and chances are the competition will never know this customer even existed. That's the real benefit of engaging the Lower 90 Percent. When your customers choose you first, they don't consider any other options.

A First Call Advantage creates competitive immunity. It circumvents the buyer's need to search for alternative solutions, and the relationship influences their behaviors. They know who to call, and trust you will deliver. Being known, liked, and trusted when a need arises means your brand can be the only one a buyer considers.

Share Interesting, Relevant Content

Engage the Lower 90 Percent of your market with interesting, relevant content. You don't have to sell to these people. Talk with them. Share ideas. Engage them in a conversation so you can get to know each other. Create content that gets people to say, "That's interesting. Tell me more." If you're sharing interesting content, it's probably valuable. And if it's interesting and valuable, you're going to build relationships. Your Brand Storylines, discussed in Principle 6, will influence the types of content that spark conversations and seed relationships.

ProVision IT, for example, engages the Lower 90 Percent with a Brand Storyline and email newsletter called "Hot Pockets." ProVision IT was founded in 2002, and it has grown into one of the predominant IT staffing firms in Ontario, Canada. The company's goal is to be an IT professional's first call when they are looking for a new job. Bob Spiers, CEO of ProVision IT, explains, "Our goal is to be top of mind when a client is looking to hire, or when an IT professional is considering changing jobs."

ProVision IT operates in a fast-paced environment, and being the first call is a powerful market position. This is where the "Hot Pockets" program comes into play. The program is designed to engage the market, especially the Lower 90 Percent, in a conversation that nurtures relationships. It's designed to build rapport and stay top of mind.

Every month ProVision IT produces a short report detailing "where are the IT jobs," and the company distributes it to clients, hiring managers, and IT professionals. The audience finds the information relevant because it demonstrates the hiring trends of their sector. For example, in its March 2014 issue, ProVision IT demonstrated the impact that winter storms were having on local hiring trends. They led with a bold title, "Hiring Freeze." The report continued, "The long cold winter was great for winter sports, but it has taken its toll on the hiring process.... Our data shows that more interviews were postponed or missed in February than normal due to weather-related issues — or because one of the parties was sick and could not attend the interview."

The information was timely and interesting, and it sparked conversations. Courtney Smith, ProVision IT's director of marketing, said, "We saw a marked increase in the 'Hot Pockets' performance in March. The report quadrupled the average click through rate to our website." ProVision IT struck a nerve. The 2014 winter was particularly hard in the northeastern United States and eastern Canada. In December 2013 the region was hit with a massive ice storm and much of Toronto and the surrounding area lost power for days. The weather-related events were top of mind, and ProVision IT could demonstrate the impact the events had on the IT job market. It was relevant information that engaged ProVision's market.

The "Hot Pockets" campaign is effective because it builds on ProVision IT's strengths. As an IT staffing firm, ProVision interviews and places hundreds of IT professionals each year. The company collects a massive amount of data on the types of jobs its clients' are recruiting for, and also on the candidates looking for jobs. By analyzing the internal data with some external market sources, ProVision IT is able to prepare relevant reports that speak to its target market.

ProVision IT draws from its core skills and assets to build relationships with the Lower 90 Percent of its market. The company has the data, and it shares it in a way that is interesting and relevant for its market. The newsletters don't have a sales pitch or a call to action, because that's not the purpose of the program. The goal is to nurture relationships — relationships that position ProVision IT as the first call when people have a need.

Play to Your Strengths

The timing has never been better for building and scaling customer relationships. We live in a golden age of marketing. You have more opportunities to connect with your customers than ever before: Facebook, LinkedIn, Twitter, email newsletters, blogging, YouTube — you name it. The choices are plentiful and the potential is immense for building relationships and growing a Sticky Brand.

Play to your firm's strengths. I'm willing to bet there are people on your team with talent you can tap into. If you have great writers, write: blog, share an email newsletter, create a guide, or write a book. If the CEO or other key members of your team are great speakers, speak: podcast, vidcast, or speak at events. If you have strong graphic designers or artists, make art: illustrations, infographics, photography, or other visual tools. Do whatever your firm can do well, and share that content broadly with your target market.

There are endless ways to engage the Lower 90 Percent of your market, and countless vehicles for creating and distributing content. At LEAPJob, one of the core ways I engaged the Lower 90 Percent was as a labor pundit on a local television station. I enjoy public speaking and TV presented an opportunity to play to one of our firm's strengths. Every month I appeared on TV to discuss the latest labor reports. I gave commentary on where the job market was heading, and insight into the North American labor market.

TV was a powerful way for LEAPJob to engage the Lower 90 Percent of our market. I'd always get calls, emails, and mentions on social networks from people who had seen me speak, and it would spark a conversation. They'd get to know me and see my point of view. And the LEAPJob brand got a big credibility bump, because we were the experts on TV. This created a First Call Advantage. When companies were looking to hire a sales and marketing professional, they called LEAPJob first. When sales and marketing people were considering a job change, they called us first too.

What can your company do to engage the Lower 90 Percent of your market? What can you do to spark conversations and build relationships? The program doesn't have to be big or sophisticated — it just has to be interesting and relevant for a non-buying audience. Opportunities to engage the Lower 90 Percent are endless. With a little creativity and experimentation, you can develop marketing programs that build relationships three years before your services are needed and create a First Call Advantage.

Building a First Call Advantage puts you in a powerful sales position. When your customers know your company, like it, and trust it, they will call you first when they have a need. Your brand skips to the front of the line, and that creates an opportunity for you to address customers' needs before anyone else.

Exercise: First Call Advantage

Objective:

Build relationships with prospects and customers upwards of three years before they have a need. Build relationships so that your customers will call your company first when they have a need.

Engage the Lower 90 Percent

Relationships take work. They require you to be proactive, engaging, and available. What can you do every month to purposefully engage your prospects, clients, and referral partners?

In the box, tick off all the items your company is already doing:

☐ Blog	☐ Webinars	☐ Speaking
☐ Email Newsletter	☐ Social Media	☐ Board Participation
☐ Direct Mail	☐ Trade shows	☐ Lunch 'n' Learns
☐ Publish Reports	☐ Sponsorship	☐ Networking
☐ Podcast/Vidcast	☐ Host Events	☐ Call to say, "hello"
☐ _____	☐ _____	☐ _____

What else are you doing? Add it to the blank spots.

Examine each of the activities you are currently conducting, and ask:

1. Is it focused on the Top 10 Percent or the Lower 90 Percent? If you mark any item as "both," look at how it can be focused to one segment or the other.
2. Are your marketing activities weighted too heavily on the Top 10 Percent or the Lower 90 Percent? If so, where do you need to shift your marketing emphasis for the next six months?
3. Which activities build and nurture relationships the best?

Develop two to four ongoing programs that are focused exclusively on the Lower 90 Percent. These could be activities you run daily, weekly, monthly, or quarterly. Build on what you are already doing, but really emphasize how those activities engage a non-buying audience, develop relationships and keep your brand top of mind.

Principle 8: Be Everywhere

Sticky Brands just seem to be everywhere. They have a buzz about them that's usually the domain of much larger companies. Unlike the big guys, they don't spend outrageous amounts of money on marketing and advertising. They stand out by growing a community.

Grow a community around your brand. Build and scale relationships so your brand is everywhere.

The Three Layers of Relationships

Growing your brand awareness starts with relationships. Your customers will not buy from you unless they like you, trust you, and find you credible. The challenge is that relationship building is time-consuming.

Until very recently, companies did not have a lot of options for nurturing and scaling relationships. They could spend a lot of money on advertising and promotions to create visibility in the hope that repetitive exposure would condition the seeds of a relationship. Or they could hire salespeople and people responsible for business development to extend their networking reach. But both options are limited, as they are dependent on time and resources.

Sticky Brands create a buzz about them because their relationships are scalable. They reach beyond traditional networking and advertising options to focus on community building. Growing a community takes the limits off how far brands can reach, and enables them to dramatically scale their impact and relationships.

Let's look at this idea a little more closely. There are three layers of relationships:

- Layer 1: Inner Circle
- Layer 2: Personal Connections
- Layer 3: Community

The first layer, the Inner Circle, is personal. These are the people who are a constant in your life. They are your family, close friends, and maybe a few key business contacts. These are the people you intrinsically know and trust. A good example of a relationship in the Inner Circle is a college buddy. You may not see him very often, but when you do it's just like old times. You pick up where you left off and the laughs continue. The Inner Circle is made up of deep relationships, and it is a small group of ten to thirty people at most.

The second layer, Personal Connections, is what we traditionally think of as our network. Each of us has between two hundred to five hundred Layer 2 connections. These are our casual friends, acquaintances, colleagues, prospects, clients, and referral partners. These are the people you know.

Companies have always focused on developing and maintaining Personal Connections because they drive business development. This is where you connect with prospects and nurture those relationships into clients. This is the layer where you form relationships with referral partners in order to develop trust and rapport with them. Your Personal Connections are the people you see on a regular basis at industry events, conferences, or even the local coffee shop. You know them, like them, and you can pick up the phone and have a conversation with them.

The challenge with Personal Connections is that there is a hard cap on how many relationships a person can maintain. It's a matter of time. There are only so many hours in the day for phone calls, emails, meetings, and other forms of personal interaction. Even if your full-time job is networking and business development, you will still hit a cap around five hundred or so Personal Connections that you can effectively maintain. As soon as you go above that number, relationships start to fall off and atrophy.

To get around the cap of Layer 2 connections, companies have scaled their networks by hiring more people. They hire salespeople, business developers, or partners to extend their reach. It's simple math. One person can maintain five hundred connections, ten people can maintain five thousand connections.

Layer 3, Community, is where things start to get interesting. This is the new frontier. Community building removes the cap on how many relationships you can maintain. Instead of being limited to a few hundred connections maintained by a select group of employees, within a community your brand can engage with thousands of people. Your company's impact is magnified because you are bringing together a group of people who are, in turn, bringing their networks. This creates an additive effect and enables a large group of disconnected people to share ideas, help each other, engage in conversations, and develop new relationships.

Focusing on the third Layer is how brands go from being small, niche players to Punching Outside Their Weight Class. It shifts them from pushing and promoting the brand to engaging a large audience with a shared experience. It takes your company beyond the confines of its marketplace, and gives it a voice that is disproportionate to your company's size.

Communities Make Brands Sticky

When you look into social media you will find countless blogs, Facebook Pages, Twitter accounts, and LinkedIn Groups that are floundering or abandoned. They are virtual ghost towns. Companies set them up with good intentions, but fail to ever get them off the ground. For example, there are over two million groups on LinkedIn,[23] but only 3 percent of them have over one thousand members. Less than 0.017 percent of groups break ten thousand members.

Vibrant, engaged, and growing social media groups are not the norm, but when a company bucks these trends it stands out like an orange tree in an evergreen forest.

Arment Dietrich is one of those firms. It is an integrated marketing communications firm, and its community, Spin Sucks, is one of the most popular PR destinations online. According to Gini Dietrich, CEO of Arment Dietrich, "Spin Sucks is one of the top three PR blogs in the world, and it has afforded us the ability to compete with the largest agencies in the world."

Gini and her team created Spin Sucks when blogging was still a novelty. "We started Spin Sucks in 2006, because we were really trying to figure out what blogging was all about," says Gini. "Twitter didn't even exist back then, and Facebook wasn't available to businesses either. But we kept hearing about blogging for business, and so we wanted to check it out. The blog has just grown from there."

The blog grew organically for the first few years, but Arment Dietrich really got serious about growing it into a community in 2009. Gini says, "2009 was our coming out year for the blog." This was the year the company changed gears and became much more strategic about what it was creating. Arment Dietrich implemented editorial calendars, search engine optimization, and dedicated employee resources to really take the blog to the next level.

Once Arment Dietrich really committed to growing it, the blog took on a life of its own. The company posts articles daily on marketing, PR, and personal development, but the magic happens in the comments. An average post will receive twenty-five to fifty comments, and some posts will catch fire and generate hundreds of comments. Entire discussions happen around each and every post. The articles are tools to spark engagement, and the community is the people who discuss them, share them, and participate in the conversations.

This is the Spin Sucks community. It is a group of people who are brought together under a shared vision. Gini says, "We're purposeful, and have a vision. Our vision is to change the perception that people have of the PR industry, and everything we do goes to that." The Spin Sucks tagline is "Fight Against Destructive Spin!" This is the company's Point of Sharing, and it's the connective glue that brings the community together. It's a shared interest to elevate the professionalism of the public relations industry, while supporting each other to develop their skills and expertise.

The Spin Sucks community elevates the Arment Dietrich brand too. The size of the community and the volume of engagement make Arment Dietrich appear to Be Everywhere. "People have the perception that we're larger than we are," says Gini. The firm has twenty-three employees, but its community has tens of thousands of members. And these people are ambassadors for the brand. They talk about Arment Dietrich. They refer to Spin Sucks. They share the content, and they invite their networks to participate as well.

Arment Dietrich Punches Outside Its Weight Class because it has nurtured an engaged community. The results are startling. Gini says, "The blog drives 80 percent of our growth." When Gini launched her second book, *Spin Sucks,* in early 2014, the community rallied around her. They helped her sell thousands of copies of the book in the first week after it was published, and the community helped her promote and get the word out in every corner of the globe.

This is the power of community. It creates an opportunity for your brand to reach and engage a much larger audience of people who share similar values, interests, and beliefs. Not everyone in the community is a potential customer, but they are active supporters of the brand. They elevate your reach far beyond networking, advertising, and traditional marketing options.

Build for Relationships

Growing a large, engaged community can create an incredible competitive advantage for your company. It delivers three key benefits:

1. Sales: The more people you can reach and engage, the more referrals and opportunities you can generate for your business.
2. Credibility: A large community is social proof that your brand is credible and delivering great services. It reduces the risk of buying from an unknown entity.
3. Differentiation: Large communities are unusual. They immediately differentiate your business from the competition because they are hard to grow, hard to maintain, and even harder for your competitors to duplicate. Michael Hyatt writes in *Platform: Get Noticed in a Noisy World*, "A good product does not stand on its own anymore. It is foundational, but it is not enough.… A [community] provides amplification. It enables you to be heard above the roar of the crowd."[24]

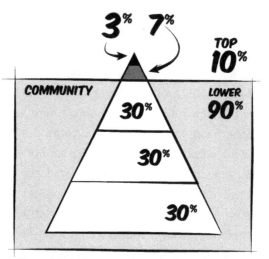

Figure 8.1: Add community to the 3% Rule. Extend
your reach, and scale your brand's relationships.

The amazing part is that growing a community builds on the work
we discussed in Principle 7: First Call Advantage. Growing a community
adds another audience for the content and ideas you are creating for the
Lower 90 Percent. In Figure 8.1 (above), you will notice a grey box surrounding the Lower 90 Percent of the 3% Rule. The box represents your
community, but it also acknowledges that these people are not customers
or prospects. They are people who have an interest in your ideas and are
actively engaged with your brand, but they are not buying your stuff.

Gini says, "We discovered that lots and lots of solopreneurs and small
PR firms know us, and are engaged in the Spin Sucks community." This
isn't Arment Dietrich's target market. Gini continues, "Eighty percent of
our clients are B-to-B, and we're venturing into some B-to-C industries
with both software and food. On the B-to-B side we do a ton of work in
manufacturing, which is one of our core competencies, as well as a lot of
work in the software as a service industry."

Even though solopreneurs and small PR firms are not going to buy Arment Dietrich's core services, they are an important part of the Spin Sucks
community. They have a shared interest in the PR industry, they are active contributors to the community, and they function as referral partners.
Gini says, "It's a very strange phenomenon where your competition say,

'Call these people, because they're the best in the business.' But it happens."
The community keeps the brand top of mind and creates a First Call Advantage. People are happy to refer the companies they know, like, and trust.

There are no limits to how far you can grow your community. Leading and building a community for your brand is the secret sauce for really scaling your company's network and reach. Traditional marketing and advertising options will plateau because you are limited by budget and resources. But a community is boundaryless. It grows organically, and the conversations and dialogue amongst the members are self-sustaining.

With an engaged community your company does not have to do all the work of promoting your brand. The community becomes a primary vehicle for growing your company's reach, influence, and credibility. It takes you from being a small brand to a brand that can compete and win against giants.

A Community Starts with 1,000 Members

Clay Shirky, author of *Here Comes Everybody* and *Cognitive Surplus*, argues that groups function best between eight and sixteen people or more than one thousand members. He writes, "Being a participant in a mid-size group often feels lousy, because you get neither the pleasures of tight interconnection nor the advantages of urban scale and diversity."

To grow a Sticky Brand you've got to look at the larger number. A few hundred followers aren't enough. You have to break one thousand members to get your community off the ground, because, as Shirky explains, "Better than 99 percent of the audience members don't participate, they just consume."[25]

Only 10 percent of an online community is active. Ninety percent of your community is silent. They don't forward articles, respond to comments, or even press the Like button. They simply consume. One percent of your audience will be actively engaged. They are the ones sparking up conversations, commenting on your articles, and recruiting new members. Nine percent of your audience are curators. They share your content through retweets, shares, and Likes, but they are not actively engaging with other members of the community.

To carry on a group conversation you need at least ten active members. They are the kernel of your community. They keep it going and make it a fun, vibrant place. Without one thousand members it's very hard to foster and sustain conversations and engagement. But getting there is hard! There are no silver bullets to achieve this milestone. It is hard slogging, and it takes time. Seth Godin, marketing guru and author of seventeen bestselling business books, says it takes "three years to build a reputation, build a permission asset, build a blog, build a following, build credibility and build the connections you'll need later."[26]

The first thousand members of your community will come from your Personal Connections. They will be people you know, and they will join because you ask them. They are there because they like you, trust you, and want to support you. For example, one of the areas I have grown my community is on LinkedIn. In May 2010 my team and I launched a small LinkedIn Group called Sticky Branding. The group started out small — five people to be exact. With hard work and focus the group has blossomed and taken on a life of its own. It's now one of the largest branding groups on LinkedIn, with over thirty-five thousand members. The group grows organically week after week, and we have members from all over the world.

I chose to build the Sticky Branding group in LinkedIn because that was a social network I was active in. When we launched the group I had around seven hundred LinkedIn connections, and it made sense to build a group where I could invite people I was already connected to. When the group launched I invited all my connections, and three hundred of them joined. This was a good starting point. I then had each member of my team do the same. They brought in two hundred more. Afterward, it was one invitation at a time.

We made a point of being active networkers — both online and offline. We attended conferences and events, followed up with old clients and colleagues, and reached out to people far and wide. It was a good opportunity to connect and meet people, but it was also the touch point to invite people who shared our interest in branding, sales, and marketing. People joined the group because they were intrigued, and they joined because we invited them. But it took time. It took us eight months of hard work to reach the first thousand members.

It's easy to get frustrated with the invitation process and try to find shortcuts like promotions and giveaways to grow your community. Avoid this temptation. To create a vibrant community for your brand you need an audience that is engaged with your content and share similar interests and values. You need people who want to be connected to you and your brand. Promotions and giveaways do not attract people seeking a relationship. They attract people seeking free stuff. You may get a surge of followers for a contest or a promotion, but it's not likely they will stick around and pay attention to your company once the promotion is over.

The secret to growing a boundaryless community is pride. Take pride in your content. Take pride in your audience. Take pride in the relationships you are nurturing and scaling. Enjoy the experience of growing your community. Your passion and excitement is infectious, and it will accelerate the community's growth beyond anything else. It will be the most effective way to get your reach past the thousand member mark, and enable your company to grow even further.

The effort will be worth it. A large, vibrant community will make your brand appear to Be Everywhere.

Communities Already Exist

Building and scaling a brand community is very powerful, but it's not the only option. You can choose to build a community, like Arment Dietrich, or you can choose to support existing ones. Both are viable options for growing your brand and reputation. The company Brilliant, for example, focuses on serving communities that already exist. Brilliant sponsors events and proactively engages associations and groups within its target markets.

Brilliant is a rapidly growing search, staffing, and management resources firm with offices in Chicago and southern Florida. The firm specializes in recruiting accounting, finance, and IT professionals for mid-sized companies. Jim Wong, CEO and founder of Brilliant, explains, "Our client focus is middle-market companies — companies that are traditionally between fifty million and one billion in revenue. We work with clients who are very interested in a partnership with their staffing providers, and view us as an extension of their HR versus just another supplier or a commodity."

Brilliant's strategy is to be the first call when its market has a need for its services. If an accountant is looking for a new job, call Brilliant. If a software developer is ready for a new challenge, call Brilliant. If a company needs a partner to find and attract these professionals, call Brilliant.

The challenge is to stand out in the crowd. The staffing industry is very competitive, and there are a lot of firms offering comparable services. Often the difference between one firm and the next is mindshare — that is, who comes to mind first when you are considering a change. Brilliant is not the only accounting and finance recruiting firm in Chicago, but it works hard to be one of the most visible. The company goes well beyond the basics of marketing and really works to engage and support its community.

The firm employs three core programs to engage and serve its communities:

1. Sponsorship: Brilliant sponsors events and associations that serve small- and medium-sized companies in its geographic markets. These can range from IT user groups to association luncheons and annual conferences. Jim explains, "We want to be involved with every professional organization that penetrates the middle market. We do this through sponsorship, marketing, and aligning ourselves with them." And on the candidate side the company is equally active. "We support up and coming accounting, finance, and IT professionals by sponsoring various scholarships through Northern Illinois University."

2. Content Marketing: Brilliant publishes weekly email newsletters that are tailored to its audiences. The company has four primary business units, and each one has corresponding email programs. The content fosters relationships, engages the Lower 90 Percent, and keeps the brand top of mind. The newsletters are sent out every Wednesday and reach Brilliant's entire database of candidates, prospects, and clients.

3. Social Media: "We are building up Brilliant's presence on the various social networks," continues Jim. "We get a number of referrals where people find us somewhere online." Brilliant places the most

emphasis on their LinkedIn and Facebook presences, because these are the social networks that both employers and job seekers are actively involved in.

Sponsorship is Brilliant's primary vehicle for participating in and supporting its communities, while the content marketing and social media are designed to reinforce and enhance that investment. Jim says, "I want us to be everywhere, or I want people to think we're everywhere." A candidate might receive the email newsletter or see one on LinkedIn, but the experience comes to life when they see Brilliant at an industry event or conference. The combination of experiences creates the impression that Brilliant is everywhere. "It builds confidence in our brand," continues Jim. "It's like, 'I saw them online, and then I saw them sponsoring our conference last month. They're everywhere.' Popping up everywhere leads prospects back to us, and it sets the condition for a sale."

"Everywhere" is relative. Mid-sized companies, like Brilliant, do not have endless marketing budgets for mass advertising and promotion. Brilliant is not going to buy its way to brand awareness with Super Bowl ads and billboards in Times Square. Creating the impression your brand is everywhere requires focusing your efforts on specific groups and communities. You don't have to Punch Outside Your Weight Class everywhere, just in the communities that have shared values and interests with your brand.

Brilliant filters communities and groups it supports in two ways: by the size of the business and by job category. As a firm, Brilliant specializes in serving mid-market companies — the kind of companies we are discussing in this book. Then Brilliant layers on the types of roles these companies hire in finance, accounting, and IT. The combined focus allows Brilliant to be very purposeful in the content it creates, and the events it sponsors.

Brilliant creates the impression that it's everywhere, because it knows who it is targeting and how to reach them. Jim explains, "I'm not too concerned if Motorola, Abbott, and Baxter even know we're on the face of the earth. But I do want to make sure that every single middle market finance, accounting, and IT professional knows about us." It's this focus that elevates the brand and makes it a go-to resource in the company's geographic markets.

People see Brilliant's generous contributions at their events, and they get to build relationships with Brilliant's team. Brilliant does not try to own the communities. Rather it focuses on being an active member and supporter of them. Brilliant's participation creates a great deal of visibility for its brand.

Serve Your Community

There is a fundamental difference between marketing and community building. Marketing is all about your company and your brand. It's about promoting the brand and finding new prospects and customers to sell to. Community building has the opposite focus: it's not about you, it's about everyone else.

The Spin Sucks community is not about Arment Dietrich, it's about marketing and PR professionals who are interested in improving their profession. My LinkedIn group is not about me or my business, it's a place for business owners, marketers, and people interested in sharing ideas and expertise on how to grow Sticky Brands. The same can be said of Brilliant. The conferences and groups it sponsors are not about Brilliant, they are about the members of those communities and their needs. Brilliant is a member of those communities, and it is doing what it can to support them.

Growing or serving a community can be perceived as an excellent lead-generation platform, but that's not accurate. Having thousands of followers engaged with your brand does not mean you can market to them. Actually, it is unlikely you can acquire thousands of followers or be a credible member of a community if you are perceived as using them for lead generation. People see right through marketing-driven communities and avoid them.

The value of a community is in its people. It's in the connections, the relationships, and the opportunities to learn and share with others. It's in the opportunities to organize and work with a disparate group of people to do something greater than yourself. Growing a community is always about the people, and it requires a shift in attitude. You don't own the community. You are a member of it. Yes, the group may be deeply linked to your brand and your people, but the second you start treating the community as a marketing platform, those relationships can dissipate.

Once a company overcomes this mental hurdle, the potential is immense. Gini Dietrich says, "Prior to launching Spin Sucks, I spent almost three years building the business without a brand or any visibility. We did that through networking and word of mouth, and the networking I was doing then was all about pounding the pavement. When I started investing in the Spin Sucks community our relationships shifted. I don't have to go to Chamber of Commerce events or cocktail parties anymore to find one or two leads. The community is a constant source of referrals."

By focusing on community building, you are focusing your company on developing, nurturing, and scaling relationships. These are the connections that grow your brand. They are the people who interact with your company and your people, and when they come across someone who needs your expertise they will refer your brand first. That's the power of community. It scales your reach far beyond any traditional marketing tools.

The 4 Bs

Growing your community to Be Everywhere takes an open mind. To focus your efforts use the 4 Bs of community building: Be Present, Be Opinionated, Be Generous, and Be Everywhere.

- Be Present: It's your community, don't get lost in the crowd. To have any impact in your community you have to be active and present in it. Make a point of initiating conversations to remain a vocal and active member of your community. Your role is to lead and demonstrate your firm's capabilities, values, and insights.
- Be Opinionated: Your company's Strong Opinions are what makes your brand interesting. Share your company's point of view throughout your community. What does your company believe in? How does it add value to your clients? How does it solve problems? Participate honestly and share your thoughts. Balanced, washed

out, and boring content never makes an impact. Let your personality shine through your content and your interactions.

- Be Generous: Help others make an impact in your community. The more people who are engaged and contributing to your community, the healthier it will be. Take a proactive stance to help people get their voices heard, questions answered, and profiles raised. When you serve your community it will give back to you in multiples.
- Be Everywhere: Make your brand highly visible in your community. Go where your customers are. Engage them online, and engage them in the real world. Look for as many areas as you can to build and scale relationships with your community.

Growing a boundaryless community does take work, but it's highly rewarding. Invest in your community, and it will reward you with greater brand awareness, more relationships, more referrals, and recognition that your company has a Sticky Brand.

Exercise: Be Everywhere

Objective:

Build and serve communities to reach new audiences and develop new relationships for your brand.

A Community Starts with 1,000 Members

Growing a dynamic community that supports your brand is a numbers game. If you don't already have a vibrant community, the first step is to get your group to a critical mass — one thousand members.

1. **Make a list.** To get your first one thousand members, start with a list of the people you know. Who are you going to invite to your community? Look at your connections on social networks to identify who you can invite to your group. Then look at your contact management system and your personal contacts to select more people to invite. Build a list and keep adding to it.

2. **Send invitations.** Make your invitations personal. People don't respond to chain messages or group emails. They will respond to you, and you alone. Craft a message that will appeal to your network. Personalize the note, and be specific with your request. Tell invitees what you are doing, what the group is all about, and why you want them to join.

3. **Go beyond the obvious.** As you exhaust your personal network, start to shift gears and consider how you can market the group to new networks. Ask your group for suggestions about who to invite. Promote the group through your marketing programs like tradeshows, newsletters, or your website. Get creative. It's hard work, but you've got to invest the effort to achieve the critical mass of the first one thousand members.

Be Visibly Active

Keep your brand top of mind by being visibly active. Every week look for one way your company can be active and engaged with your community.

There is no one size fits all answer. It's up to you to find meaningful ways to engage your community, build relationships, and deliver value to the people around you.

Principle 9: Pick Your Priorities

The number one value of growing a Sticky Brand is sales. Sticky Brands sell more, faster — provided they are purposeful with their resources. Small- and mid-sized companies don't have vast marketing budgets and resources to move the sales needle.

To drive sales and grow a Sticky Brand, focus on one priority at a time: Volume, Velocity, or Value.

How to Eat an Elephant

How do you eat an elephant? One bite at a time. The same goes for branding. Growing a Sticky Brand is a process. It takes an enormous amount of time, resources, and work to grow your company's brand so it stands out above the herd and has a sustainable competitive advantage. You're not going to do that in 90 or 180 days. It's a process.

Many companies treat branding as if it were a one-time event. For example, they may find their website is out of date and they need to overhaul it to reflect the current state of their business. When branding is treated as a one-time event, a website overhaul follows a predictable trajectory. As soon as the website starts to get updated, plenty of other branding projects start to pop up. The logo and identity get revised, and that triggers a redesign of all the letterhead and business cards. Then all the copy on the site needs to be rewritten with a refined value proposition and better stories, and that triggers a redesign of the brochures and sales documents. Then the executive biographies turn out to need work too, and that triggers a photo shoot. What started as a small, inexpensive project can quickly balloon into a massive rebranding effort. It's like a home renovation. You start with your kitchen but soon you're renovating the whole house.

It's unnecessary to go through these costly, all-consuming rebranding projects. You don't just brand your business and then leave it for five years until it breaks again. Growing a Sticky Brand is a process, not an event. It's far more effective to view branding as a process of continuous improvement and treat it like a Total Quality Management (TQM) program. By making incremental improvements you can continuously enhance the business, the customer experience, and your competitive advantage. Priorities are key when you apply a TQM mindset to branding. It is truly a process of eating the elephant one bite at a time.

The 3 Vs

To grow a Sticky Brand, make deliberate decisions. Choose your priorities. What does your business need right now? What about in twelve, twenty-four, or thirty-six months? Where is your business headed and how do you need your brand to perform?

These are broad strategic questions, but they are essential for focusing your company's time, attention, and resources. You cannot do everything, so what is the most pressing need?

Sales is a primary measure of success, and an area your brand can directly effect. Almost all marketing initiatives can be tied to a core sales metric, what I call the 3 Vs: Volume, Velocity, and Value.

- Volume: Increase customer demand and generate sales ready leads.
- Velocity: Improve your sales closing rate by accelerating your customers' buying process.
- Value: Reduce price sensitivity and increase the perceived value of your products and services.

The 3 Vs help to define your sales and marketing efforts and set the priorities for your brand. They help to clarify how your brand will perform to support your business goals.

Let's break down the 3 Vs in more detail, and discuss when to apply them.

Volume: How Often Does the Phone Ring?

The ultimate measure of a Sticky Brand's performance is customer inquiries. How often does your company receive inquiries for your products and services? Is your brand consistently pulling in new customers? This is Volume. It is the amount of demand for your products and services.

Companies tend to prioritize Volume when they are in growth mode. To achieve their growth goals they focus on generating more brand awareness and increasing the number of sales opportunities.

Volume was my number one concern following the rebrand of my family's business to LEAPJob. We needed the brand to drive sales for two reasons. First, we were suffering from sales purgatory because we had repositioned the business and were growing our reputation and awareness in a new market. Second, our sales team was too dependent on generating sales inquiries from networking, cold calling, and referrals. We needed the brand to do the heavy lifting. Our priority for the brand was getting the phone to ring: Volume.

By being very clear about our priorities we could make purposeful decisions about our sales and marketing. We focused our efforts on activities that generated new relationships, developed brand awareness, and positioned our business as the first call when a client had a need. The focus was liberating. There are always hundreds of things you *should* be doing, but what *must* you do? We could free ourselves of the *shoulds*, and focus on the activities that generated customer inquiries.

Volume is relatively easy to measure: the number of inquiries your firm receives in a given period. You can track this metric in a contact management system like *Salesforce.com* or Microsoft CRM, an Excel spreadsheet, or with pen and paper. How you capture the information isn't important as long as you are able to effectively collect and measure the demand for your products. Being able to track your performance allows you to create new goals, measure achievements, and develop the strategies to increase Volume for your business.

At LEAPJob we tracked inquiries-per-month with a goal of acquiring one new customer per week. We captured the information in our contact management system and looked at the reports weekly. We examined how each marketing activity we implemented moved the Volume metric, and we constantly monitored how our sales and marketing efforts were performing. This helped keep our team focused and accountable to the priorities of the business.

Volume is relative to every business. We all need it, but how much can vary widely. How many inquiries do you need to move the sales needle? Inquiries can be tracked by quarter, month, week, day, or even hour. It depends on your company's average-size sale and how many transactions your company needs to hit its revenue targets. If Volume is your priority, how many inquiries do you need to generate to move the sales needle forward?

To increase Volume for your brand, consider the big picture. A trap many companies fall into is looking at their marketing activities in isolation. They could look at the outcomes of an individual trade show and say, "That didn't generate enough leads. It wasn't worth it." Hold on a second. That is not quite true. Evaluating your marketing activities in isolation does not demonstrate if you are increasing demand.

You cannot see the forest for the trees if you evaluate your marketing activities in isolation. Each and every marketing activity may not tangibly increase Volume, but how the programs work together is what drives your brand's performance. Trade shows and social media campaigns are tactics. They are the building blocks of your company's sales and marketing. Each tactic on its own may not demonstrate a clear impact on Volume, but each one may be an integral component of the overall strategy.

Measuring tactics are a weak indicator of your marketing performance. Focus on the strategies and goals your company is striving to achieve. Group your marketing activities into buckets: trade shows and events, sponsorship, media relations and PR, digital marketing, advertising, and so on. It is far easier to manage and measure a group of marketing activities to see the overall impact on Volume.

With clear goals and strong metrics, you can develop the strategies and programs necessary to make your brand appear to Be Everywhere, and that will drive interested buyers to your door.

Velocity: How Quickly Do Your Customers Buy?

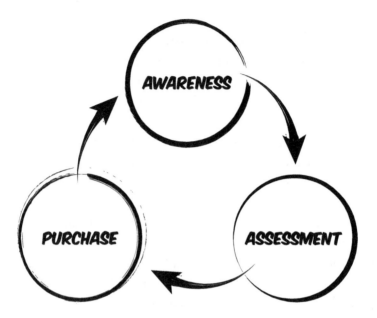

Figure 9.1: Customers go through three predictable buying stages:
Awareness, Assessment, Purchase.

Velocity is the speed a customer travels through the buying cycle.

When you analyze your customers you will discover they go through three predictable buying stages: Awareness, Assessment, and Purchase (see Figure 9.1). The predictability of your customers' buying habits is why you can develop structured sales processes and metrics.

1. Awareness: In the first stage the customer experiences a trigger event or situation that sparks a need. In the recruiting industry the triggers are often employee turnover, a new project, or a surge in growth. The company faces a situation where it needs to add or replace talent and has to go to market to source new employees. What are the trigger events in your industry? What situations or symptoms do your clients face that bring them to market and have them consider their needs?

2. Assessment: In the Assessment phase your customers are considering

their options. Who are the suppliers? What products do they offer? Are there any new or creative ways to solve the issue, or do they continue to work with the tried-and-true suppliers? What are the costs of switching, and is it actually worth moving forward with this project? This is usually the time a customer goes through all your marketing material and engages your sales reps. They want to know how your company can help. This is also a critical time, because they may decide to shelve the project if they determine the options aren't right or are too expensive. The Assessment phase is when customers are kicking the proverbial tires.

3. Purchase: Once the customer commits to the project they narrow down their selection and move forward with the purchasing process. This is the actual sales process: negotiate, define contract terms, and buy. This is the stuff salespeople live for, but it's also an exciting moment for the customer. They've made a decision, and they are moving forward with it.

Velocity tracks how quickly a customer moves through the buying process. Since we are not mind readers, and may not know when a trigger event occurs, we track Velocity from inquiry to purchase.

Companies focus on Velocity when they are optimizing their business or brand. This is a valuable set of metrics to consider when your brand is in transition, such as Tilting the Odds or developing Function That Resonates, or when you are trying to make your value proposition more sticky. Velocity demonstrates what areas of your brand are working and what are not. By identifying problem areas, you can focus on improving them so customers are able to make buying decisions more efficiently.

Versature, who we discussed in Principle 7: First Call Advantage, has a full-time business analyst on staff who is responsible for improving the Velocity of their digital marketing. She is an expert in Google Analytics and Google AdWords, and her job is to continually analyze and adjust the company's online presence to make sure it comes up at the top of Google searches when customers are looking for the services Versature offers. Paul Emond, CEO of Versature, says, "It's important to track every interaction from introduction to customer. We have our tracking down to a science, and continually adjust our SEO and AdWords campaigns for peak performance."

Versature's business analyst has been instrumental in improving the performance of the company's digital marketing through 2013 and 2014. Paul explains, "Historically we have invested ten thousand dollars per month on Google AdWords, but through Lisa's work we have reduced our spend by 40 percent while increasing the number and quality of the leads we are receiving."

Versature defined Velocity as a priority for its brand. Rather than spending more money on lead generation and awareness, the company focused on optimizing that spend. Versature asked the question, "How can we do this better?" And it set about improving its marketing performance.

To measure Velocity, analyze how your customers buy and their decision points along the way. For example, the first step might be when a prospect finds your website on Google and fills out an inquiry form. Then you can move forward with an introductory call, schedule product demonstrations, present a proposal, sign a contract, and deliver your services. In the example I quickly presented there are seven steps, or conversion points, in the buying process.

Conversion points provide an added layer of insight, and they demonstrate how your customers are moving through logical stages in the buying cycle. For example, how long does it take a customer to move from completing the inquiry form to receiving a product demonstration, and then demonstration to contract, and contract to delivery? What percentage of your customers do not convert at each point? Are customers getting stuck or stalled at any key points in the process?

Time and conversion metrics are valuable because they function as an early warning system of problems that might be occurring in the buying process. They help you optimize and improve your brand. Can you make your messaging clearer? Can you improve the buying experience? Can you enhance or adjust your products to better serve your clients? Can you reduce friction at any of the conversion points?

Velocity is your priority to improve the overall buying experience and make it easy for your customers to buy your products and services.

Value: Are Your Customers Willing to Pay a Premium for Your Brand?

One of the biggest yet often overlooked benefits of growing your brand is competitive immunity. It's hard to compete and win against a Sticky Brand. Value is a priority to reduce your customers' price sensitivity and increase your company's competitive immunity.

You can see the benefit of improving the Value of your brand by looking at the laptop market — how Apple competes with the Windows computer manufacturers. Apple has a great deal of competitive immunity, while Dell, Toshiba, and HP are fierce competitors. The PC manufacturers compete on price and features and regularly try to undercut each other. Apple, on the other hand, operates relatively unscathed because its brand insulates the company from the competition.

Improving the Value of your brand does more than generate sales. It creates a competitive advantage by protecting your company from direct competition. It keeps your competition at bay like a moat around a castle, and it insulates and protects your products and services in measurable ways:

- Increased perceived value and affinity toward your products and services.
- Increased customer attraction and retention. Your customers seek out your brand, and come back frequently.
- Decreased price sensitivity, because your clients choose you first and gravitate toward your brand.

Apple, for example, earns fourteen times more profit per laptop than their PC competitors. Apple's average sale price of MacBooks in 2013 was $1,229.56, with an assumed profit margin of 18.9 percent. The average sale price of the Windows PC manufacturers in the same period was $544.30, with an average profit per PC of 2.73 percent, or $15.71.[27]

Apple is an anomaly in business. Very few companies will ever achieve such an enviable brand position. But the profit gap between Sticky Brands and their competitors exists in every sector. By prioritizing the Value of your brand, you are choosing to grow a recognized brand and become the category leader.

Let's look at another example from the mid-market. In 2008 Neatfreak made the choice to increase Value by growing a brand. Today Neatfreak is the category leader in home organization and storage. It designs and manufactures storage products for closets, garments, shoes, and laundry. You can buy the company's solutions from major retailers like Walmart, Target, and Bed Bath & Beyond. But prior to 2008 it was a supplier. Neatfreak was like the Windows PC manufacturers duking it out with their competition on price.

The company was founded in 1977 as Varimpo, a private label manufacturer of plastic hangers and other storage products. The company was a successful manufacturer, but to get to the next level it decided to become a brand. Neatfreak placed its emphasis on the Value priority, and took purposeful steps to create a brand that stood out in the marketplace. John Collins, chief marketing officer of the Neatfreak Group, explains, "We were playing the private label game, but we asked ourselves how do we create a compelling opportunity for A, the consumer, and B, our retail partners?"

Neatfreak was born out of a desire to drive growth and profitability of the company by improving the Value of the brand. A supplier is just that, a supplier. A brand has more freedom to innovate and design products that delight consumers, while creating programs that move products off the store shelves, which delights retailers.

The company enhanced the Value of its products by being purposeful about how it served its customers. John continues, "Our purpose is to help keep the consumer organized, and control the chaos in their life. We bring harmony to everyday life, and we do that through imaginative products." Design is at the heart of fulfilling the company's purpose, as well as how it fundamentally moved the Value metric. The private label companies are effective at manufacturing, but Neatfreak stays a step ahead with its commitment to design. Design radiates through all aspects of the brand, from Neatfreak's products to its packaging. John explains, "53 percent of the decisions in this category are decided on packaging. We spent a lot of time and money repositioning Neatfreak on store shelves, because once a customer experiences our products the repurchase rate is extremely high."

Measuring Value can be more laborious than Volume or Velocity, because you are comparing your brand with your competitors. You are considering how your business is positioned and if customers are willing to pay a premium for your products and services. Measuring Value is all about considering how you elevate your brand out of the competitive fray and build direct relationships with your customers — relationships where your customers choose you first, and are less price-sensitive.

Neatfreak can measure Value based on market share, product positioning on store shelves, and placement of its products and branding in store flyers and promotional materials. The company can also evaluate its brand performance based on consumer behaviors. How well is the brand known? What is a customer's propensity to seek out their products again? Are customers willing to pay a small premium for the products over private label options?

By prioritizing Value, Neatfreak transitioned from being a private label manufacturer to being a brand. This was a challenging transition — Value is the hardest of the 3 Vs to move. It takes far more than effective marketing and promotions to create competitive immunity. It requires strategy, product innovation, and making decisions across the organization to improve the company's performance.

The brand is the mark of credibility and trust. By improving Value you are making choices that lift your company out of the competitive fray, to become the leader of your niche.

The Right Metrics Drive Success

Driving the 3 Vs requires metrics — measurements that clearly show if your sales and marketing efforts are working and if your brand is achieving its goals. As the old adage goes, "You can't manage what you can't measure." The challenge is choosing the right metrics.

There is no shortage of data to manage your business with, but not all metrics are equal. The number of Likes your company's Facebook Page receives or the virality of a social media campaign may seem impressive, but what do they prove? If they don't support one of the 3 Vs you may be focused on a vanity metric — a feel-good metric that doesn't offer clear insight or guidance on your brand's performance.

Good metrics are simple. This was driven home for me a few years ago at a family business conference I attended. One of the speakers was the president of a third-generation distribution company who recounted the story of how his Dad used to monitor the health of their business. Every day around three in the afternoon his father toured their facility. He went around the warehouse and chatted with the employees. It was his opportunity to connect with the staff and take the pulse of the business. His final stop was the loading dock. He'd walk out into the parking lot and count the trucks.

The speaker said, "My father had a simple formula for managing the business. A truck in every loading bay meant we were growing. Empty loading bays meant tough times were coming." The company had a variety of accounting and sales metrics to draw from, but counting trucks was his predictor of success. "My dad could spot a budgeting problem or a turn in the economy before our accountants did, based on his daily inspections," said the speaker.

Counting trucks was an effective metric to manage Volume. It was a tangible way to see the company's sales performance, and didn't require digging into sales reports and customer orders. It was a visual metric that he monitored daily. It's simple, actionable metrics like counting trucks that drive the 3 Vs.

When you focus on one of the 3 Vs, choose a few very direct ways to measure performance. Volume relies on metrics related to lead generation and brand awareness. Velocity has metrics related to time, win ratios, and overall sales performance. Value is measured by market share, profitability, and how often you have to discount or compete on price to win new business. There are lots of ways you can measure the 3 Vs. Choose the metrics that are most relevant for your business and your priorities.

One V at a Time

It's very hard, if not impossible, to focus on all 3 Vs at once. Each is a big priority and consumes a lot of resources. Prioritize your Vs and work on one at a time.

Through my ten years at LEAPJob our priorities oscillated through the 3 Vs. We may have started with Volume, but we spent a lot of time working on Value and Velocity too. For example, we reduced our sales cycle from sixty days to two calls. We achieved this by making our website sell as well as our best salesperson and by developing a very effective sales process. Our salespeople could qualify a lead from our website in twenty minutes, and be able to reinforce our value proposition and get the customer excited with our capabilities. At the end of the call they would email a service agreement to the customer and schedule a followup call to address any questions. The second call was a "closing call."

Improving the efficiency of our sales process became a priority because we had spent so much time working on the Volume priority. We had increased the demand for our service, and the phone was ringing consistently. We had to work smarter, and we could be selective on the clients we worked with. This gave our sales team confidence. They were proud of the services they sold and clear about how we worked. That confidence resonated in the customer meetings, which further enhanced the Velocity of the buying process.

Pick your priorities annually. At LEAPJob we defined our priorities every year and re-evaluated them every six months. We did this through a formal strategic planning process. During the last sixty days of our fiscal year we began planning for the year ahead. We reviewed our accomplishments, evaluated our position in the marketplace, set our goals, and defined which of the 3 Vs was most pressing for the upcoming fiscal year. We made a point of working on one V at a time.

The 3 Vs are there to support your business and your overall strategy. What is your company trying to achieve this year and how do you need your brand to perform? Are there areas of your brand that are holding your business back? Where do you want your business to be in three years?

Pick the priorities that will make the most impact on your business.

Exercise: Pick Your Priorities

Objective:

Focus on one priority — Volume, Velocity, or Value — at a time. What does your business need to focus on for the next six months?

What's Holding You Back?

What's holding your business back at the moment?

- Sales: Do you need to generate more opportunities?
- Quality or size of customers: Are you selling to the right customers?
- Winning deals: Does your sales team struggle to close deals? Customers come to you, but they seem to get cold feet at some point.
- Price: Are you suffering from death by a thousand cuts? Do you have to constantly discount to win business?
- Resources: Are you drowning in opportunities, and need to use your resources more effectively?
- Competition: Are you facing a competitor that's beating your brand up, and making it hard to win?
- Something else: There's a clear threat or problem holding your brand back.

Analyze your business and the areas that you need to fix in order to accelerate your growth. Identify one or two pressing needs every six months and make a plan with clear goals, resources, and metrics to fix those issues.

One V at a Time

You only have so many resources to grow your brand. Focus on one V at a time. Every six months evaluate the state of your business. Start today by asking:

1. What is your priority for the next six months?
2. How will you move that priority? What's the plan?
3. What's your measures of success?

Your priorities will help you determine which V is most pressing. Focus on that V and develop a plan to make measurable improvements on it over the next six months.

Part 4: Over Commit, Over Deliver

Desire is the key to motivation, but it's the determination and commitment to unrelenting pursuit of your goal — a commitment to excellence — that will enable you to attain the success you seek.
— *Mario Andretti, world champion racing driver*

Sticky Brands are built from the inside out. They have Big Goals, dynamic cultures, and strong values that drive them to outperform their peers. They've got an attitude to serve their customers better than anyone else.

Your brand gains energy by serving your clients and delivering tangible value. Focus your company on what it does best and where it delivers the most value.

In this section you will learn how to:

- Build your **Brand from the Inside Out** by developing a dynamic corporate culture that is deeply committed to your clients' success.
- Create a culture that is **Proud to Serve,** because your duty is to serve your customers and deliver incredible experiences.
- Build your brand using **Big Goals and Bold Actions** by getting your team committed to Big Goals that propel your company to innovate, serve clients, and deliver exceptional services.

Principle 10: Branding from the Inside Out

Sticky Brands are built from the inside out. Their people, culture, and values all come together to foster innovation and deliver remarkable client experiences.

Your company's people, culture, and values are the glue that holds it together. Those strong bonds enable your company to attract the right employees and serve your clients even better.

It Takes More than Talent

Andrew Carnegie said, "Take away my people, but leave my factories, and soon grass will grow on the factory floors. Take away my factories, but leave my people, and soon we will have a new and better factory."

Carnegie's quote speaks to the power of talent. When you have the right people you can achieve great things. Jim Collins echoed this sentiment in his book *Good to Great*, "Those who build great companies understand that the ultimate throttle on growth for any company is not markets, or technology, or competition, or products. It is one thing above all others: the ability to get and keep enough of the right people."[28]

Talent is universally recognized as an essential ingredient of growing a successful business, but it takes more than just good people. CEOs love to say, "Our people are our most important asset." It's one of the most overused phrases in business, and many companies' actions do not support the claim. Companies proclaim their people are important, but are quick to lay them off when times get tough.

Great talent is not enough. Companies with Sticky Brands have great talent, but so do average companies. There are lots of examples of this in sports. Well-funded teams acquire all-star talent but fail to achieve their potential. For example, the U.S. Men's Basketball Team at the 2004 Olympics was stacked: Dwyane Wade, LeBron James, Carmelo Anthony, Tim Duncan, and Allen Iverson. But the team failed to gel, it was pushed out of gold medal contention after losing three matches in the tournament and had to settle for a bronze.

Well-funded companies can hire and attract high-caliber talent, but that does not mean they will grow a Sticky Brand. What separates the Sticky Brands from everyone else is how they organize and focus their talent to perform to a higher standard. They bring together their people, culture, and values as core assets of the company.

The metaphor of the three-legged stool is apt here. If any of the legs are weak or too short, the stool will be unbalanced and fall over. Companies with Sticky Brands outperform their peers because they have invested in their human resources: people, culture, and values. They have purpose, well-defined values, a dynamic culture, and the right talent to effectively serve their clients. They can beat better-funded and bigger companies because they are more focused and work better together. They have a team that outperforms the competition.

Sticky Brands are built from the inside out. Your team and the way your people work together is what ultimately enables your company to serve its clients and grow into a Sticky Brand.

Bake Values into Your Brand

Sticky Brands have a heightened awareness of their values and culture. They are very self-aware. They know who they are, why they exist, and who they serve. Customers pick up on this self-awareness and confidence. It radiates through the brand and demonstrates a business is committed to serving them.

WildPlay Element Parks lives and breathes its values. It's what makes the parks so much fun and brings clients back again and again. The company creates and operates outdoor activity parks with unique aerial adventures such as bungee jumps, zip lines, and aerial courses. The parks are situated in picturesque areas and encourage people to participate in nature-based recreation.

On the surface you may think the parks are designed for adventure seekers. Bungee jumping is not for everyone. If you are afraid of heights or the thought of jumping off a 150-foot bridge gives you the willies, you are probably not going to beat a path to WildPlay's doors. But that's not what the parks are all about. Tom Benson, co-founder and CEO of WildPlay, explains, "From the very start of our company we knew our purpose: to get folks out of their comfort zone as a catalyst for change." It's this singular purpose that shapes WildPlay's brand and the way it runs its business.

The bungee jumps and zip lines are the tools that support WildPlay's purpose. Customers come back because they have fun and learn to overcome something they didn't know they could. At the end of the experience the staff will often hear clients say, "I was afraid ahead of time, but not afterwards. The experience taught me [and they will insert a personal story]." That shift in attitude is the kernel of the WildPlay brand experience.

To consistently deliver on its purpose, WildPlay has codified its core values:

- Evolve the Guest: Aim to anticipate and exceed the expectations of guests.
- Nurture the Clan: WildPlay's family works together as a creative and tight team where dependability is a given.
- Taste the Dirt: If you don't know Mother Earth, you won't take care of her.
- Share the Fruit: The labor of the business should result in an obvious and tangible benefit to its community.

This is just a snippet of WildPlay's values. The values are expanded or contracted to fit the situation. More importantly, everyone on the team believes in and lives these values.

WildPlay incorporates its values into everything it does. They are ingrained in the company's hiring, training, and management processes. They are embedded in its messaging, both internally and externally. You will find them on WildPlay's website and you will hear about them in company meetings. Tom continues, "Whenever we have an important decision to make we pull out our core values. It influences our decision making process."

WildPlay bakes its values into the language, culture, and processes of its business.

Values are very personal. Many companies use trite words like "integrity" and "excellence." Those words may sound professional, but they are hollow. Enron, for example, had four core values: Respect, Integrity, Communication, and Excellence. Published in its 1998 annual report, Enron described what "Respect" meant to the company: "We treat others as we would like to be treated ourselves. We do not tolerate abusive or disrespectful treatment. Ruthlessness, callousness, and arrogance don't belong here."[29]

The values may have looked impressive in the annual report, but they were just marketing copy. Enron went bankrupt in 2004 following revelations of massive, systemic accounting fraud. It was one of the largest bankruptcies in U.S. history. The company's four core values were not guiding principles or tools for the employees. And I doubt Enron's management team used the core values to support important decisions like WildPlay does.

The effectiveness of WildPlay's values is in the specificity of how they are written and linked to the business's purpose. The language is uniquely its own. Instead of using words like "delight" and "excellence," WildPlay talks about "evolving the guest." The full description of that value reads, "To anticipate and exceed the expectations of guests, we seek out and create challenging opportunities to ensure they have an empowering, transforming experience. We deliver the thrill of primal fun and games through best-of-breed practices and no one gets hurt. *Life is not lived to fullness in a comfort zone.*"

Values come alive with rich language. Anyone on WildPlay's team can speak to the four values and what they mean. They can talk about it in their own language, but also draw on the language of their culture. "Primal fun and games" may not mean much to you and me, but it carries weight and meaning for WildPlay's staff.

The specificity and relevance of the values also supports WildPlay's growth. The company is expanding rapidly and opening new parks thousands of miles away from its head office. Even though the new parks are geographically isolated, WildPlay is conscientiously working to reinforce and replicate the culture and values — what makes its current park experiences so sticky — at each new site.

Tom describes the company's approach to replicating the values at the new parks as being like "splitting a sourdough starter." Sourdough bread is unique, because it's alive. If maintained properly the starter can last for years. Bakers make loaves from an original batch of dough called the "mother." They break pieces off the mother to create "children," and this is what maintains the unique flavor of each new loaf of sourdough.

As WildPlay grows, it is treating its culture and values with similar care. It is alive, and an integral part of the brand. With each new park the team works to split off the culture and values from the original parks — the mother — and infuse the new ones with it. The goal is to not only create a consistent client experience at each park, but to create a consistent employee experience and value system.

The people, culture, and values are what differentiates WildPlay. The barriers to entry in the adventure park industry are fairly low. It does not require a lot of capital to build zip lines, bungee jumps, and aerial courses. WildPlay are not the only park operators, but the client experience between operators can be drastically different.

It's the people, culture, and values that give the activities purpose and create compelling client experiences. WildPlay's staff is organized with a clear purpose, "Be a catalyst for change." Every day the company takes its clients out of their comfort zones in a safe and fun environment and creates an opportunity for personal development.

That experience brings clients back again and again, and you can see it in the makeup of the company's clientele. Many park operators are dependent on tourism, and have seasonal businesses. WildPlay bucks this trend by creating an experience that draws "locals" to them. The experience is more than a thrill. It is an opportunity to challenge yourself, and grow in the process.

What are your company's core values? Have you codified them so everyone on your team knows them and can speak to them? Do you use your values to guide your major business decisions?

Happy Employees Create Happy Customers

Your values are closely linked to your corporate culture. David Cronin, CTO of DevFacto, argues, "Happy employees create happy customers."

A happy employee brings your brand to life. It's hard to miss people who truly love their jobs. That passion is infectious and you can see it in the care and commitment they bring to their work. When your employees love their jobs and love coming to work, it goes a long way to making your brand sticky.

DevFacto is an IT consulting firm, and its purpose is to "build software that humans love to use." The company combines its purpose with deep expertise in a wide variety of technologies, such as mobile and Web application development, and it creates systems for companies in a variety of sectors across North America and Europe. The company is on a growth tear. DevFacto has grown over 96 percent in the past three years and is featured as one of the "Top 10 Canadian Mobile Technology Companies" in the Branham 300 list.[30] But if you ask David what makes DevFacto unique, he will tell you it's the company's culture.

DevFacto's commitment to culture is part of what it is. Since its founding in 2007, the company has always placed a premium on its employees. David says, "The two most important aspects of our business [are] our culture and our people." It's not lip service when David says "employees are our most important asset." DevFacto puts its money where its mouth is. The company strategically invests in its culture, and that becomes obvious when you visit DevFacto's offices.

The office is designed for creativity. Each employee has their own office. David argues that creative work requires focus and the ability to work undisturbed. But when the staff come out into the main office, they are greeted with a space designed for interaction and collaboration. The office has meeting spaces and bump zones to foster human connections.

The bump zones are an important part of the DevFacto culture. The employees are a social group of people, and face-to-face interactions amongst the team members supports their purpose. For example, the lunchroom is in the center of the office, and everyone eats there daily. Final interviews with potential employees are conducted in the lunchroom. The candidates have an opportunity to interact with the individuals on the team as they are coming and going, and they conduct mini interviews on the spot. The lunchroom interviews give candidates a chance to experience the company culture, and the team is able to participate in the hiring process.

A strong culture is managed and nurtured. DevFacto supports communication and camaraderie with regular activities. It has daily team huddles to catch up and discuss projects, and every Friday the music gets turned on at four o'clock for "Beer Time." This is a social moment for the team to interact with one another, celebrate the week's successes, and rejuvenate.

The firm also goes well above and beyond industry norms to reward its team. For its fifth anniversary the company took the entire team to Las Vegas to celebrate. David explains, "If you're not living it, you don't get it. Most companies would never dream of spending a couple hundred grand on a party for their staff. It would get denied every time [it was] requested, because it costs too much money. We feel it's so integral to our culture that we invest in it."

Investing in your culture is a value. You either believe in it, or you don't. DevFacto's commitment to culture reflects the beliefs and values of its founders, David Cronin and Chris Izquierdo. "If we were building this company for sale we would have done things differently," says David. "We wouldn't throw the parties, or have the offices we do. But we're building our company so that our employees can buy it from us in the future. That's our plan. We are building a culture that people love so much they are willing to put their own money into it."

That is a profound idea: create a business your employees love so much they can't imagine anyone else owning it. It is a very worthy ideal to aspire to. But let's look beyond the employees to consider the brand too. Imagine how your customers feel when your employees believe in your company so much they are willing to personally invest in it. That commitment elevates the brand in the customers' minds, and delivers a sticky experience.

Every client interaction is an opportunity to demonstrate what makes the firm unique. "Everybody is truly happy to work here. We're inspired by each other, and that aids in our word-of-mouth marketing, and having customers that come back," says Laura Browning, DevFacto's marketing specialist. The culture increases DevFacto's reach and is a key driver for business development. They do not have to rely on a handful of elite consultants or salespeople to grow the firm's brand and reputation. The culture is doing a lot of the heavy lifting. The firm has over seventy full-time employees and forty subcontractors. Each person is an ambassador of the firm, and clients come back again and again because they prefer to work with these people.

A strong culture creates a self-fulfilling prophecy: "Happy employees create happy customers." It's a treat to work with enthusiastic and committed people. It fosters creativity and enriches relationships. Employees are a Sticky Brand's greatest asset. They not only do the work they are tasked to do, they go above and beyond the call of duty. They are brand ambassadors and they form deep client relationships based on the good work they do. Your people are what give your brand meaning and substance in the minds of your customers.

Relationships Make Brands Sticky

Even if you can't differentiate your brand with your products, you can differentiate it with your people.

Claude-André Pouliot is the president of Macpek, one of North America's largest distributors of truck parts. Claude-André explains, "The way our industry is built is extremely competitive. In truck parts, we cannot differentiate ourselves with our products, because the products we have could be found at ten other distributors. We cannot say, 'our product is better than yours,' because it's the same product. It's coming from the same manufacturer, it has the same part number, it has the same everything. So one of the primary ways we differentiate ourselves is with our relationships with our customers, and finding ways to get closer to them."

One of the ways Macpek gets closer to its clients and suppliers is through community events. For example, the company celebrated its fortieth anniversary in 2014 with a 320-kilometer (200-mile) relay race from Mont Tremblant to the company's head office in Quebec City. Claude-André continues, "Each of the participants ran ten kilometers four times, which is the equivalent of a marathon in a forty-eight hour period."

Macpek's leadership team announced the idea for the relay at their 2013 Christmas party and were extremely surprised with the level of engagement. "We employ one hundred and seventy-five people in total, and sixty-five decided to join up. And that's people from all over the company, not just corporate. We have people participating in branches as far away as a ten-hour drive from here. At least one person per branch registered for the event," says Claude-André.

The event supports a corporate philosophy of having "a healthy mind and a healthy body," but it is also an excellent platform for building and nurturing client relationships. Macpek's goal from the start was to get five hundred people to cross the finish line. Claude-André explains, "We involved our customers, our suppliers, our families, and our friends. People registered online for a twenty-, ten-, five-, or a two-kilometer race, depending on their interests and abilities."

The event exceeded expectations. Fifty of Macpek's employees ran the full marathon, and over 650 people joined them at the finish line. It was an exciting way to finish the race. "Ten kilometers from the finish line three hundred people joined the marathon runners, and at the five kilometer mark another three hundred joined us. It was very inspiring and emotional," says Claude-André.

The event was amazing for the chemistry of the business. It invigorated the passion, respect, and camaraderie of the team. The employees trained together every week, and it created a buzz that travelled well beyond the walls of the company. The company involved the community and the event became a lightning rod to reinforce Macpek's brand in its marketplace. The story got picked up in the press and the company was featured in newspapers, trade magazines, and even the local radio station.

It's this passion and the relationships they nurture that elevate Macpek's brand. Claude-André says, "We are perceived as being different, because we like to engage people. We want to build relationships with our employees, customers, and vendors at the heart level. Instead of being only about numbers and brains, we want them to emotionally know us better."

Those personal connections separate Macpek. The company's people and its relationships are an asset for the business, and they differentiate Macpek from its competitors. Customers choose Macpek first because they have a personal connection with the company and its employees. "At our core we are a service business. We happen to sell truck parts, but we are really a service company first," says Claude-André.

Relationships are a powerful differentiator because they are very human. People buy from people — they buy from people they know, like, and trust. The more active your employees are in their community, the more relationships they will form. Not only will customers seek out your corporate brand, they will seek out the people they know, like, and trust. Relationships provide an added layer of depth and trust, which will bring your customers back again and again.

Your People Shape Your Brand

People with the right talents are a vital part of growing a Sticky Brand.

Talent is the throttle for your brand. When you work with passionate, engaged people who have the right talent, it's like stepping on the gas. It's surprising how far and fast you can go. But if talents are misaligned, your company's performance is stunted. It's like driving on bald tires. You just can't get traction — there is always something holding you back no matter how hard you step on the gas.

Peter Drucker wrote, "Results are obtained by exploiting opportunities, not by solving problems." It doesn't matter how much money or resources you have at your disposal. A talented group of people committed to serving their clients can spot more opportunities and outperform much bigger competitors.

Your people, culture, and values are a constant in your business. They are the root of your business, and they give it strength as you continually adapt and grow your brand to better serve your customers. John Smale, former CEO of Procter & Gamble, said, "There are some important things that haven't changed during the course of this company's life and that is the basic character of this institution. Our values. The things that reflect our basic principles…. These are the things that make P&G a great company. And these are the principles that will last, in my judgment, as long as this company lasts through the ages."

It's easy to give lip service to your people being your company's most important assets, but Sticky Brands elevate human resources as a clear competitive advantage of their business. Your company can't Over Commit and Over Deliver with a mediocre team. You cannot innovate and challenge the status quo with a disengaged team. You need everyone in your organization focused and committed to making your company as good as it possibly can be.

Branding isn't just about marketing. It's about creating an organization that is purposefully built to innovate and serve its clients.

Exercise: Build From the Inside Out

Objective:

Invest in your company's people, culture, and values to attract the right employees and serve your clients even better.

"We Are Not ... "

Developing your company's core values can involve a lot of navel gazing and trying to define what you believe and why. So flip the exercise on its head and consider what you are not.

Gather Your Team

This is a team exercise and is best completed with five or more people. Bring your employees together and give each of them a pad of sticky notes and a pen. If you don't have five employees, recruit some colleagues and friends to assist you with the activity.

Seven Statements

Ask each member of your team to write seven "We are not ... " statements — one per sticky note. For example, "We are not pushy salespeople." Or, "We are not the lowest-priced option."

Arrange the Sticky Notes

Task one member of your team with arranging her seven sticky notes on a wall. Place them horizontally to create a row.

Group the Seven Statements

Once you have the first row on the wall, ask each member of your team to place their Seven Statements. Create columns with the sticky notes. If a statement is similar or the same as one already on the wall, place the item below it. If it's unique add it to the right of the top row to create a new column.

The Dominant Columns

Which columns have the longest lists? Identify the longest two or three columns. These lists provide a glimpse at your values. The long lists represent values or beliefs that your team cares deeply about. They are things your company does not stand for. They are areas to avoid.

Reverse the Statements

For each of the dominant statements consider the positive side of the "We are not … " statement. Frame the value in a positive light. What is the opposite of the statement?

Once you have a list of positive statements, try to rework them into three to six core values. Make the statements actionable and descriptive. For example, "We believe [and fill in how the positive statement applies]." These are values that reflect what your company believes, what is important to your team, and why your company operates the way it does.

Principle 11: Proud to Serve

The people who grow Sticky Brands are filled with pride. They take a great deal of pride in their work, their customers, and the results they deliver. And it shows. They cultivate adoring customers because they are deeply committed to the work they do.

Pride is powerful. It propels your company to innovate and deliver exceptional services.

Be Brilliant at the Basics

The best things in life are simple, authentic, and real: real food, real craftsmanship, real customer service, real products. They all have a quality that trumps the latest fads and trends — they are true to their essence.

In Steve Jobs's biography by Walter Isaacson, Jobs recounted a story of his father's approach to craftsmanship. Jobs's father spent as much time crafting the back of fences and cabinets as he did the front. Jobs said, "He loved doing things right. He even cared about the look of the parts you couldn't see." This attention to detail allowed his work to stand the test of time.[31]

Sticky Brands share a similar trait. They aren't simply serving a market need, they go a step further. They create products and services that are functional, well-designed, and just work. There is a timeless quality to their services, because Sticky Brands sweat the little things. They don't ship buggy, partially finished products or sell poorly executed services. Their attention to detail is absolute, and it radiates through their products, services, hiring practices, operations, marketing, and every customer touch point.

Companies with a Sticky Brand behave more like artisans than factories.

The basics may not be glamorous or exciting, but they are essential. It is the work that goes on behind the scenes that makes a product or service great. And it's the little things that clients remember and appreciate: an employee who was friendly and served them well, a product that is incredibly reliable and never needed maintenance, a product innovation that anticipated the customers' needs. These simple yet highly functional experiences create a sticky factor, and the more you deliver these experiences, the more your customers will come back.

This focus on the basics is a source of pride for Sticky Brands, and it's rooted in their purpose. Sticky Brands have a higher calling, and that propels them to innovate and reach further. Yvon Chouinard, founder of Patagonia, described his vision for his company's clothing, "You should be able to wash travel clothes in a sink or a cooking pot, then hang them out to dry in a hut and still look decent for the plane ride home."[32]

Yvon Chouinard was an elite-level mountain climber and outdoor enthusiast. He used his experiences in that sport to ensure that Patagonia's clothing was right for his peers. He wasn't in business to simply turn out a comparable competitive product. He was driven to create products that would stand up to the rugged conditions on the side of a mountain. This purpose and pride drove Patagonia to challenge the status quo and develop products for a devout customer base.

Pride is an essential ingredient in growing your brand. With a clear purpose that you take pride in, there is always a right way and a wrong way. Not all business is good business, and not all decisions are driven by the bottom line. It's pride that gives you and your team the fortitude to make hard choices — choices that align with your business's purpose and the needs of your customers.

When your clients know your company does the right things consistently, they won't need to look anywhere else. Revisit the first section of this book, Position to Win. The basics are the building blocks of your business and are centered on where your company plays and how it wins. What do your products or services deliver? Why do your clients need them? How can you be just a little bit better?

It's not sophisticated, but often the basics are the hardest part of business.

Good Is Not Enough

We all work with plenty of companies that do a good job. They are efficient, effective, and deliver good value for the price. But good is not enough. Good is average, and average is not worth bragging about.

Pizza Nova is not satisfied with being good enough. It defines "quality" as the core differentiator of its brand, and it's at the heart of the company's client experience. Pizza Nova is a regional pizza chain representing over 130 locations in southern Ontario. Domenic Primucci, president of Pizza Nova, explains, "Our success is directly attributed to our commitment to the quality of our products, and the incredible team of people that represent Pizza Nova. Together, we pride ourselves on the simple fact that we deliver quality, and our customers can taste the difference."

Quality is a challenging attribute to market, but it is a deep source of pride for Pizza Nova. And that pride has cultivated high customer expectations. Customers become conditioned to the quality of service, and find themselves disappointed when they try another option. Pizza Nova capitalizes on those expectations, and has been building on them for over fifty years.

The company was founded in 1963 by Domenic's father, Sam, and his uncles, Mike, Joe, and Vince. The brothers started out with a single pizzeria and worked hard to introduce their market to pizza. Domenic explains, "In the early sixties pizza was a relatively new concept." The Primuccis created a loyal customer base by combining traditional Italian cooking, great service, and high-quality products. People loved the experience, and it fostered growth in the early years.

Pizza Nova's heritage radiates throughout the customer experience, and differentiates its products from the herd. The family's Italian roots influence its recipes, products, and approach to pizza, and its commitment to customer service has been a main focus of the business for over fifty years. And those roots are a source of pride and they cultivate adoring customers. When there is endless choice in a marketplace, you have to give your customers a reason to seek you out and choose your brand first.

Pizza Nova believes the heart of its customer experience is quality. Domenic says, "We do not take our product lightly. Let me put it this way: When you construct a building there is a foundation. Our company's foundation is our products, and the foundation of our core product, pizza, is the dough, sauce, and cheese. Those are the three mainstays of the pizza, and then everyone customizes it with the toppings they want: pepperoni, peppers, mushrooms, or whatever they like. But our dough, sauce, and cheese have to be the strongest they possibly can be. And we build a strong base — a strong foundation."

Domenic is clear where quality starts: the dough, sauce, and cheese. That foundation sets the standard for Pizza Nova's brand and how it approaches all others aspects of the business. Domenic continues, "We want to ensure that it is a good quality product, because our customers are loyal and understand that anything we bring out is going to be a great product."

That's it. That's the essence of Pizza Nova's purpose and how they cultivate adoring customers. For over fifty years the company has conditioned the trust and expectation that it will deliver a product that is consistently better. You can get a good pizza anywhere, but Pizza Nova gives you one you really appreciate.

Pizza Nova has built on this expectation and developed quality as a core value of the company. For example, when the company selects and evaluates new products, it considers three criteria:

1. Is it better than what the company is currently using? This may sound straightforward, but Pizza Nova has clear standards for its products, and what is required to improve on them.
2. Is it at the right price point? Pizza Nova has a defined niche and target market with price expectations.
3. Is it consistent? With over 130 locations, Pizza Nova works to create a consistent customer experience across all of its establishments.

These criteria set the expectations for the business. To maintain the loyalty of its customers, Pizza Nova has to continually raise the bar and stay true to what brings customers back. The product may be commonplace, but the experience is not.

The company also validates that it is performing to peak potential and developing brand loyalty. Pizza Nova applies feedback loops to engage its customers and ensure the company is exceeding expectations. Domenic explains, "We have a Customer Courtesy Call program [in which] we try to call a lot of our first-time customers. We try to call them back the next evening and learn about their experience. When we call we don't get into a big long survey. We value our customers' time. All we say is, 'Hi, this is Pizza Nova calling, and we would like to know how your pizza was last night?' That's it. That's all we ask."

The calls are incredibly effective. Many customers are shocked to receive the call because companies rarely follow up with their clients after a purchase. Domenic continues, "Once the customer gets over the initial surprise, most open up and share their impressions. We are always surprised [by] how much information people are willing to share. It is very revealing."

The call program generates a lot of valuable insight for Pizza Nova. Not only does the company hear about problems and issues that might have occurred, it also hears about all the good things it does. Pizza Nova has created a feedback loop to learn from its customers, and that helps the company focus its resources so it can continually improve the quality of its products and services.

The calls also work to reinforce the customer experience. A customer may purchase the pizza on a whim, but the call reinforces the Pizza Nova brand. The calls demonstrate the company's commitment to quality and customer service, and it goes a long way to reinforcing relationships with new customers.

At their core, companies with Sticky Brands understand what makes them unique, and they live it, breathe it, and own it. It's more than marketing spin. It's a source of pride. It is who they are, and that is evident to their customers. Each time a customer returns, the relationship is reinforced, and soon the brand is their only choice.

Love Your Customers, and They'll Love You Back

Customer service is another source of pride for Sticky Brands. They are not satisfied to simply serve. They Over Commit and Over Deliver to cultivate adoring customers that sing their praises.

I witnessed the power of adoring customers at the Family Business Forum in April 2013. The Forum brings together CEOs and leaders of successful family businesses to share their stories. Larry Rosen, the CEO of Harry Rosen, was one of the presenters at the event, and he told the audience his company loves Muldoon's Coffee.

Larry Rosen wasn't there to talk about Muldoon's. He was there to deliver a talk on the success of his business. Harry Rosen is the largest retailer of designer menswear in Canada, with sixteen locations conducting over $230 million in sales annually. Larry took the time to acknowledge Muldoon's Coffee as Harry Rosen's coffee supplier, and showcased how Muldoon's quality and service reinforce the Harry Rosen brand.

Larry's endorsement was a spur-of-the-moment statement. The Muldoon brothers had presented a few hours earlier, and it was a fitting acknowledgement. It also spoke to the deeper relationship between these two companies. The Muldoon's service was on Larry's radar, and he could speak to his company's relationship with its supplier. The comments were genuine and unscripted.

That is the added bonus for taking pride in customer service: your customers will talk about you. Happy customers are your greatest salespeople because they can explain how they use your services and what they appreciate. Spontaneous, genuine customer endorsements are extraordinarily valuable and they carry a lot of influence. They're also not very common. We don't go around bragging about all the companies we purchase from on a daily basis. There are too many to mention, let alone think about. The companies we endorse behave differently. They create an experience that places their products and services into our frame of reference, and they become a topic worth talking about.

Muldoon's gets onto peoples' radar with a high-quality service, great-tasting coffee, and the application of their Brand Storylines (see Principle 6: "That's Interesting. Tell Me More."). But the company cultivates adoring customer relationships by going a step further — Muldoon's is very proud to serve its customers. Shaun Muldoon, CEO of Muldoon's Coffee, explains, "We love our business. We love what we do. We are so involved in everything my people do and my company does, because we believe in it. As we grow the business, I don't want to be twice as big, but half as good. That would just be such a disappointment for everyone involved."

Jimmy Muldoon, president of Muldoon's, complements those sentiments, "If you see my people on the street you will see the exact same attitude." The attitude is ingrained in the culture at Muldoon's, and everyone is committed to delivering exceptional customer service.

In one of my interviews at Muldoon's I saw the team roll into action when they received a customer complaint. A long-term customer called Jimmy to discuss some issues with their account, and the whole tone of the company shifted on the spot. It was like someone flipped the switch, and the office was under DEFCON 2. All that was missing were flashing red lights and sirens warning of imminent danger.

The client had recently hired a new operations manager who was re-evaluating all the company's service providers, and Muldoon's was on the list. The complaints were relatively minor, but you wouldn't have known that watching the Muldoon's team. The service manager was digging through the system, pulling up reports. The customer service reps were being called to verify information. The account manager was running around the plant talking to people and collecting information. All of the client's complaints were being attended to with the utmost care.

Shaun explains, "These are opportunities for our business to get better. We cannot afford to get lax in our systems or delivery as we grow. We are growing quickly, and have the tiger by the tail. A call like this forces our people and systems to improve so we can consistently deliver the level of quality we expect."

"In our business, our current customers come first. When there's an issue or a complaint from a client, everything stops," says Shaun. "It doesn't matter how much is in the sales funnel, or the next customer we are about to win. We serve our current customers first, and make sure they are satisfied."

The Muldoon's attitude might seem over-the-top, but it is an integral part of what the company stands for. Muldoon's responds to its customers, because everyone in the company takes pride in the business and their client relationships. Their clients are loyal and happy to sing their praises as a result. The company is growing quickly because its customers are fans.

This story is not unique to Muldoon's. The companies featured in this book all demonstrate a commitment to customer service. To paraphrase Shaun, they love their customers and they love what they do.

Listen and Respond

Pride is not one-sided. Pride wells up in Sticky Brands because they know the work they are doing matters. It's not an ego trip to create a brilliant product or service. Pride is found in the results a Sticky Brand delivers. They purposefully serve their clients and respond to their needs.

To effectively serve your clients you have to listen. My sixth-grade teacher, Mrs. Dixon, used to say, "You were born with two ears and one mouth. Use them in that proportion." This is an applicable guideline for your company too. It's hard to innovate if you are not listening. Paying attention to your clients' needs and ideas generates so many good opportunities to serve them better.

Phil Hollows, CEO of FeedBlitz, explains, "We are very engaged with our clients, and we know many of them personally. We go to their events throughout the year, and we spend a lot of time listening to them." Feed-Blitz is a content distribution company. They help bloggers and businesses get their content out to their audience via email, RSS feeds, and social media updates. The service automates the process and makes it easier to get content — articles, blog posts, and newsletters — into customers' hands.

FeedBlitz is competing with giants in its industry. Its largest direct competitor is Google's FeedBurner service. FeedBurner provides a free alternative for managing a blog's RSS feed and sending email updates to subscribers. Phil continues, "The only way we can compete successfully against free services like Google is by out-servicing our clients and out-listening our competitors."

If you are paying attention, your clients will tell you what they want and need.

FeedBlitz has carved out a strong niche amongst professional bloggers and publishers. It has a who's who of "A-listers" working on its platform: Copyblogger Media, Chris Brogan's *Owner Magazine*, *SimplyRecipes.com*,

Fred Wilson of Union Square Ventures, and many more. These companies could have their needs filled by the giants in the industry — Feed-Burner, Constant Contact, MailChimp — but these savvy publishers are choosing to work with FeedBlitz.

Listening and being responsive is a source of pride for FeedBlitz. Phil says, "It's not just the product or the functionality. It's our organization. It's an attitude. Our people live and breathe this stuff. They talk the language of our customers, and are really committed to serving them better."

Dialogue not only builds relationships, it creates understanding. As you build relationships you gain insight and understanding, and that creates opportunities to respond. For example, FeedBlitz used the 2014 New Media Conference (NMX) in Las Vegas to solidify its product direction for the upcoming year. Phil explains, "We went into the conference with a decision to make. As an organization we were wrestling with three strategic directions that we could take for the year, and they were all very viable options. Honestly, there was no wrong choice. So we were struggling to determine which direction to go in. Within the first ninety minutes of the exhibition floor being opened and talking to the people at NMX, the decision became simple. The message was repeated by multiple different people from multiple different backgrounds, and it was obvious what we had to do."

The decision wasn't made at the boardroom table. It was made by talking with customers and listening. "Just turning up and listening and being available is a huge competitive advantage, and it's what we do," says Phil.

Listening is attitudinal, and for many companies it does not come naturally. But for Sticky Brands listening is a source of pride and a primary way of fulfilling their purpose. If they didn't listen, it would be very hard to proactively address their clients' needs. Companies with Sticky Brands listen and respond, and that cultivates customer loyalty.

The Craftsman's Mindset

No one ever developed adoring customers by being average. It takes a commitment to do something outstanding. It takes purpose, vision, and pride in your work. It takes a craftsman's mindset to grow a Sticky Brand.

Craftsmen spend years, if not decades, honing their craft. Malcolm Gladwell popularized the concept of the 10,000 Hour Rule in his book *Outliers*. The rule was developed by Anders Ericsson, a researcher and professor of psychology at Florida State University, who specializes in the field of expertise. Ericsson determined expertise is formed through deliberate practice:[33]

> To people who have never reached a national or international level of competition, it may appear that excellence is simply the result of practicing daily for years or even decades. However, living in a cave does not make you a geologist. Not all practice makes perfect. You need a particular kind of practice — deliberate practice — to develop expertise. When most people practice, they focus on the things they already know how to do. Deliberate practice is different. It entails considerable, specific, and sustained efforts to do something you can't do well — or even at all. Research across domains shows that it is only by working at what you can't do that you turn into the expert you want to become.

It takes time and commitment to get better and to reach a point where your company can be considered world-class experts. Do you have that level of commitment? Do you have the purpose and pride to push your team to develop their skills and capabilities to consistently improve and serve your customers? Is your work a source of pride?

Becoming a Sticky Brand is an expression of having your company live and breathe its purpose. How else will you be able to commit the time and effort to this process? Becoming an expert is a hard and difficult road, but that process is also extremely fulfilling — it's a source of pride. Sticky Brands thoroughly enjoy the work they do, and the people they serve. It fuels them to grow a company that stands out in a crowded marketplace.

Exercise: Proud to Serve

Objective:

Create feedback loops to monitor and manage your brand's performance. Pay close attention to how your company is performing so you can Over Commit and Over Deliver for your customers' benefit.

Feedback Loops

How is your brand performing? How do you know if your company is doing well (or not)? Without quantifiable customer feedback, all you have are opinions and hearsay on how well your company is performing.

Create feedback loops to monitor your brand's performance and listen to your customers. Develop a feedback loop in five steps:

1. **Determine what your company takes pride in.** What are you striving to deliver? This is the focal point for an effective feedback loop. Measure what is most important to fulfill your brand promise to your customers.

2. **Develop a short survey to measure your point of pride.** Craft one to five simple, direct questions to ask your customers how your company performed. Pizza Nova asks one question, "How was your pizza last night?" What questions can you ask that are direct but open-ended to solicit customer feedback?

3. **Distribute your survey.** You want to know what your customers think. Find the best time to engage your customers for feedback, and apply that process to as many customers as possible. If at all possible, survey your customers over the phone or in person. An online survey can only tell you so much.

4. **Publish the results of your feedback loop for your team.** Make them highly visible. Place the results where everyone can see them. Feedback loops are most effective when they are visible, everyone understands their meaning, and they can act on the results.

5. **Schedule quarterly action meetings.** The point of collecting this data is to use it. Schedule a meeting every quarter to review the

results of the feedback loops, and develop action plans to improve performance. Use this data to make your business even stronger and your brand stickier.

Sticky Brands take customer feedback seriously, because they provide accountability. Your customers will tell you what they want, and they will tell you how your company is doing.

Principle 12: Big Goals and Bold Actions

Sticky Brands make Big Goals and take Bold Actions. Their goals energize the brand. They create momentum and excitement around a business that is infectious. People are excited to talk about the company, refer others to it, and buy from it, because of its accomplishments.

Ratchet up the energy and excitement in your company with Big Goals and Bold Actions.

Energize Your Brand

A growing, vibrant company is infectious. There is a buzz about it. People see the success and they are intrigued. People want to work for them and other companies want to buy from them. An energized brand is an exciting brand.

But where does that energy come from?

It's internal. There is a fire that burns from within that drives an organization to innovate, challenge the giants of its industry, and grow its brand. Sticky Brands are driven by Big Goals and Bold Actions — they have a purpose to be something greater than they are. These goals act as a rallying cry, and direct your team on where to focus its efforts and energy. Big Goals engage your people — they reach out and grab hold of them, because they are tangible and highly focused. Your people get the Big Goals right away, and that energizes them.

This energy is potent. It differentiates your business, because your team behaves differently from the competition. They are bolder, more proactive, and more action-oriented. This makes your company appear bigger, more innovative, more attractive, and more desirable.

David Aaker writes in *Brand Relevance*, "Whether you make hot dogs or market insurance, it is hard to conceive of new offerings that are going to energize the marketplace. So the need is to look beyond the offerings for ways to make the brand interesting, involving, dynamic, enthusiastic, and even a topic of conversation."[34] One of the primary ways small- and mid-sized companies energize their market and make their brand more interesting is by accomplishing their Big Goals.

Goals come in all sizes, but they have one thing in common. They create energy. With the right goals you can shift your brand from being average to sticky. Steve Jobs lured John Sculley from Pepsi-Cola to Apple with a legendary pitch, "Do you want to sell sugared water for the rest of your life? Or do you want to come with me and change the world?" He set the stage with an aspirational goal: do you want to change the world? The question is relevant for your company too. What is your company striving for? To paraphrase Steve Jobs, how is your company going to make a dent in the universe?

Grab hold of and commit to your Big Goals. They energize your brand and drive your company to grow further, faster.

Break Through Revenue Plateaus

There are not many people who can walk into a gym for the first time and bench press three hundred pounds. It takes time, effort, and training to develop the skills and strength to move that much weight. The process is filled with ruts and plateaus.

Businesses face a similar dilemma. Small- and mid-sized companies hit predictable revenue plateaus as they grow: $1 million, $5 million, $10 million, $25

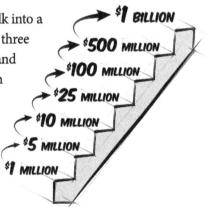

Figure 12.1: Small- and mid-sized companies grow through predictable revenue plateaus.

million, $100 million, $500 million, $1 billion (see Figure 12.1). At each
level their growth can slow down or stall — to break free of these plateaus
involves a major shift for the business.

It all starts with a choice: a commitment to grow. In 2010 Richard
Resnick and Gireesh Sonnad merged their small IT consulting practices
to form Silverline, a *Salesforce.com* implementation partner. Salesforce is
a global software company that is best known for its customer relationship management (CRM) product. But *Salesforce.com* is far more comprehensive than CRM, and encompasses a wide variety of software tools
for businesses. Companies engage Silverline to help them set up, config-
ure, and customize *Salesforce.com* to work for their business.

Today, Silverline is one of the fastest growing *Salesforce.com* partners.
Rich explains, "We noticed that all the other competitors in our space
were getting caught up at the five-million-dollar mark, or less, and they'd
have ten to twenty people. That is where the majority of the firms in our
space are operating, and we decided we could do better than this. We
wanted to grow this thing, and figure out how to push forward. As soon
as Gireesh and I made that agreement things really started cooking."

Since its founding, Silverline has doubled in size every year — both
in revenue and employees. It has rocketed through the first three revenue plateaus. By the start of 2014, the company employed over one
hundred people.

Breaking through revenue plateaus requires investing in the infrastructure of the next level. It often feels like you are throwing the baby
out with the bathwater as you push through each plateau. The team, systems, and approach that got you to $1 million are not the same at $10 or
$25 million. Rich explains, "Many companies in our space get stuck at
the $5-million mark, because most of them are not willing to take the
time and effort that's required to build the processes around scalability
— developing the processes that allow you to scale."

To get to the next level, a $5- to $7-million business needs to invest
in the infrastructure of a $10-million business. Once the systems, talent,
and resources are in place, the company can experience a growth spurt
and burst through the plateau. The process repeats itself as they charge
toward the $25-million level.

To break free of your current plateau, you must develop the capabilities of the next level. This is an ideal opportunity for applying Big Goals. Big Goals focus your attention on where to take your business. You don't need to apply a lofty goal that sounds great on paper but is meaningless to your staff and customers. Commit to goals that will make a tangible impact on your business right away.

On a regular basis, take the pulse of your business by asking three questions:

1. What systems or processes do we need to reach the next plateau?
2. What do our customers want and need?
3. Are we committed to breaking through the next plateau?

For Big Goals to be effective they need to be anchored on the needs of the business and what it will take to develop the systems, talent, and infrastructure for the next level.

It is a process of constant evaluation and commitment. Rich says, "Annually, we do a gut check and ask, 'Are we still doing the right thing? Do we still want to keep growing the way we are growing?'" These are important questions, because scaling a company is hard work and puts a lot of strain on the business. "Every year as the numbers go up we have to re-evaluate our goals. Now where we are, it's a bigger undertaking then we've seen before. We are training leaders and managers who have never had to lead or manage before, and getting them comfortable with that. And we are working to make them successful. This is probably the hardest thing we've done."

As difficult as it is to break through the revenue plateaus, it's an important ingredient for growing a Sticky Brand. Silverline's growth is proof of their capabilities. There are over 650 *Salesforce.com* consulting partners in North America, but Silverline has a First Call Advantage in two niche markets: financial services and health care. The company's reputation drives a lot of its sales. "Almost 90 percent of our business, or our lead flow, comes from *Salesforce.com* itself," says Gireesh Sonnad.

"While *Salesforce.com* is attempting to sell a customer on the Salesforce platform, especially in our vertical markets, they look for partners who have done it before or can help prove to these customers that what they are trying to achieve can be done within the Salesforce platform," continues Gireesh. "As a result, a huge majority of our lead flow comes from Salesforce looking for partners to meet their customer needs, and then recommending us to them."

Silverline's capabilities and market position support its First Call Advantage, but the company's growth is also a major contributor. There's an energy surrounding the firm. It is constantly growing, winning awards, working with new clients, building relationships, and doing things its competitors are not. The buzz around the firm keeps its brand top of mind with the *Salesforce.com* sales reps who refer Silverline to their clients. A salesperson cannot remember the names of all the partners and each firm's strengths and weaknesses, but they will remember the partner that is growing and innovating faster than anyone else.

Sticky Brands are not stagnant. They are aware of the revenue plateaus and the importance of getting to the next level: reaching and serving more customers. If you do really great work and really believe in your products and services, growth is an important factor for fulfilling your company's purpose. By increasing sales and growing the company, you are reaching more customers, more markets, and helping even more people succeed. It is a goal worth pursuing.

Deciding to grow a Sticky Brand and breaking through the revenue plateaus always starts with a goal. What do you want to build? Are you satisfied with where your company is today, or do believe you can do better?

Make Big Goals Aspirational

Growing a Sticky Brand is more than breaking through the revenue plateaus and chasing sales targets. Driving top-line growth is an important measure of success, because it demonstrates you are fulfilling your brand's potential and reaching more and more people. But your team needs to understand why the goals it is working toward are so important.

Big Goals engage both the heart and the mind. They have meaning and they inform your staff how to perform and what it is working to achieve. For example, in the early years of Starbucks, Howard Schultz set out to innovate in the coffee shop category by making Starbucks a "third place between work and home." This was a clear statement that guided the organization to create a retail experience that encouraged consumers to treat Starbucks as a community destination.

Your Big Goals are a lens. A well-crafted goal is aspirational and motivating. It drives action because it helps your team understand what they are working to achieve. Starbucks' staff can evaluate if new programs, food options, or promotions support the goal of creating a "third place." If they do, the team can execute them. If they don't, the team can make quick decisions and move on to more productive work.

To develop your Big Goals, make them SMART. SMART is a mnemonic device, and it's a useful tool for creating effective goals. It stands for:

- **S**pecific: The goal focuses on a specific area of your organization or business. For example, Silverline has clear goals to develop managers and leaders as it pushes toward its next revenue plateau. Gireesh and Rich are investing in the firm's HR capabilities to support their growth objectives.
- **M**easurable: An effective goal can be measured, and you can quantify progress. You need to answer the question, "How will we know when the goal is accomplished, and how do we know if we are on track?"
- **A**chievable: If the goal is not attainable, it's not a goal. It's a dream. Unachievable goals undermine your credibility because it becomes evident to your team that working toward them is a waste of time.
- **R**elevant: What's the meaning behind the goal? Why is it important for the business, brand, and customers? Your team needs to understand the "why" behind every big goal.
- **T**ime-bound: There is a clear timeframe for the goal. It has a beginning, middle, and end date. Some goals may be very large and take two to three years to complete, others may be completed in a few weeks, but they all have a conclusion. You are working to achieve the goal by a specific date.

All five criteria are important for developing effective goals, but I find Relevance is the most important aspect for branding. When a goal is just about a number, it lacks the human element to drive action.

Companies tend to gravitate toward numeric Big Goals, but fail to add a human or aspirational quality to them. Management might say, "We want to grow by X percent this year." "We want to increase our market share to Y level." "We want to acquire Z new customers per month." There is nothing wrong with these isolated numeric targets, but they require an aspirational component to engage your team and propel its members to change their behaviors so they can reach greater heights. Isolated numeric goals on their own are not enough to grow a Sticky Brand.

Isolated numeric goals present two obstacles. First, they are hard to convert into action. What does adding a few more customers really mean? Why does the growth rate really matter? Second, isolated numeric goals tend to backfire with rank-and-file employees. If they do not understand what they are working toward, they may view the purpose of growth as simply for increasing the executives' bonuses. The biggest problem with isolated numeric goals is that they are all about you, not your customers. Big Goals build brands when they are focused on serving your customers. That focus is what is aspirational, motivating, and engaging for your people. Focusing on your customers creates energy and growth.

Roger Martin writes, "Starbucks, Nike, and McDonald's, each massively successful in its own way, frame their ambitions around their customers. And note the tenor of those aspirations: Nike wants to serve every athlete (not just some of them); McDonald's wants to be its customers' favorite place to eat (not just a convenient choice for families to go). Each company doesn't want to serve customers; it wants to win with them."[35]

The Principles discussed in this book are all linked to your company's aspirations. Who is your company? Who does your company serve? What makes your firm unique? Why does your company do what it does? There is always a deep-seeded belief and vision that propels companies to grow Sticky Brands.

When you develop Big Goals, really consider the R, Relevance:

- What will achieving the Big Goal mean for your customers?
- How will achieving the Big Goal change your industry and the way business is conducted?
- Why is it important for your company to reach this goal?

These are the questions your employees need answers for. The numeric goal may sound great at a company meeting, but its residual impact is limited. The number does not engage your employees' hearts. It does not tell them how to act or why they should change their behaviors. Sticky Brands have deep and personal aspirations.

Big Goals Drive Bold Actions

"We exist to help our customers solve problems," says Paul Kerr, CEO of Scalar Decisions. Scalar is an IT solution provider that architects, implements, and manages mission-critical IT systems. But what Scalar does is only part of the story. The company stands out in the IT services industry because it is growing faster than its competitors, working with a who's who of clients, and constantly expanding into new markets. In ten years the company has grown to over $140 million in revenue, and it has been featured in the PROFIT 500 list, which is a listing of Canada's fastest growing companies, five years in a row. Paul says, "To get on the PROFIT list once is relatively easy, but getting on there four or five years in a row is fairly tough to do because you need consistent, high growth."

Driving this level of growth requires a multi-faceted approach. As Paul explains, "Velocity of customer acquisition is how we got to $140 million. We've had a ruthless dedication to being great at customer awareness and branding, opportunity identification to help clients find and solve problems, and then selling and bringing these opportunities to a close." Scalar has a culture of sales, but from the external perspective it's a customer-driven culture. "Our customers are the reason we exist, and our job is to service them," continues Paul.

Staying true to its purpose plays an important part in Scalar's growth. Paul warns, "As companies scale and grow they risk losing the plot. 'Losing the plot' means thinking something that doesn't matter one iota to our customers should be important to us for some reason."

This is an excellent way to describe purpose, and it pulls everyone back to focusing on what is most important for the customer. Paul continues: "I will say it twenty times a week, 'Guys, we're losing the plot.' And now they know what I mean. We are not considering this challenge or issue from our customers' or prospective customers' lens. We are doing something for the sake of business, someone's political aspirations internally, or because it's our bias. This can't happen. We have to continually stay focused on what is most important: our customers."

Helping customers solve complex IT infrastructure challenges is Scalar's purpose. Growth, sales results, and scale are the results, not the purpose. By fulfilling its purpose, the company has set the conditions for its customers to choose Scalar first and come back again and again. Then Scalar layers on its ambition and Big Goals to drive the company forward.

"We're phenomenally goal-oriented," says Paul. "Every week we met as a leadership team, and only looked at our six key goals for the fiscal. For last year the goals were linked to product revenue, professional services revenue, managed services revenue, EBITDA [Earnings Before Interest, Taxes, Depreciation and Amortization] before variable pay, accounts receivable, and employee satisfaction. We focused on these goals, because we believed all of them drove top-line revenue, growth, and profitability overall." These are broad categories, but Scalar shaped them into very specific goals that are directly connected to its customers. The company defined where it was heading, and the goals shaped the behaviors and actions the organization needed to achieve them.

Based on Scalar's size, the goals are parceled out for specific groups in the business. The executive team focuses on the big picture, whereas the departments are tasked with specific objectives that support the organization in achieving its Big Goals. Paul says, "In [fall 2015] we've identified IT Security as a key market to develop. We have a team of twelve to eighteen people that are focused almost exclusively on that sector. Their goal is to achieve twenty-one million dollars next year, and that's all they think about." By segmenting its goals, Scalar is able to empower its various teams to not only grow the business, but to be very focused on a specific set of customers and their unique needs.

Big Goals are only valuable if they drive actions. Scalar grows faster than its peers, because the priority is on acting, not talking. "I love having goals in place, driving towards them, getting them accomplished, and then setting new goals," says Paul. "But there's a big difference between setting and working towards goals, and sitting around in the sandbox and only talking about strategies." Bold Actions grow brands and businesses, not dreams. If you don't work toward and accomplish your goals, the strategies and ideas behind them are meaningless. Big Goals are nothing without Bold Actions.

If It Ain't Broke, Break It!

Sticky Brands are constantly reinventing themselves. Partly because that's how they defend their brand and drive growth, but also because it's part of the makeup of the business and the people inside it. Jeremy Moon of Icebreaker says, "I've never defended the status quo. I feel anxious if we are not in a constant process of reinvention. People that become too attached to the status quo or resist change never survive long at Icebreaker. We need fluidity to evolve." Jeremy is the chairman and creative director of Icebreaker, and calls this process of reinvention "shedding our skin."

Every two to three years Icebreaker does a complete evaluation of its business and what it needs to do for the next three years. Jeremy says, "The process we use is the process of reinvention. Every two to three years the team and I do a teardown of the business, and I do the same for myself as the CEO. We work out what is the design of the business — where are we and where do we need to move towards? What's working, and what isn't working? Who here is part of the team going forward, and who has stopped growing and can't keep up? In what areas have I stopped growing? Who do I need to be for the team and the company going forward? It's very cathartic, but this process has happened many times."

Icebreaker is an outdoor clothing designer and manufacturer headquartered in New Zealand. All of its clothes are made with merino wool. Merino is a breed of sheep that live in the Southern Alps of New Zealand, and their fleece is very different from that of regular sheep. It's not sharp or scratchy like normal wool. It is exceptionally soft and lightweight, and ideal for outdoor sports clothing because it's breathable in the summer and insulating in the winter.

Today, Icebreaker is a global brand. Its products are sold in more than four thousand stores in forty-four countries. They have nineteen company-branded retail stores, a robust e-commerce platform, and over four hundred employees worldwide. And the company is on a growth tear — sales have tripled in the past six years to over two hundred million dollars.

This level of growth is quite remarkable when you consider the company was founded in 1994 and no one had ever sold merino wool outdoor clothing before Icebreaker. When Jeremy Moon founded the company merino wool was a novelty. It was only used in high end suits like Armani, and companies were not using natural fibers in long underwear. Those garments were made with synthetic fibers like polyester.

Jeremy saw the potential in the wool and developed a business plan to grow an international brand. This was the first goal. He says, "From the very start, the purpose was to build an international business from New Zealand. That goal framed all my decisions." Over the years the company has gone through constant reinvention to bring its clothing to new markets and more people.

Jeremy explains, "In 1999 I had to shift from only being about local sales to having to develop international teams and markets. It happened in 2003 when I shifted our manufacturing base, not the wool production but the manufacturing, from New Zealand to Shanghai, where the best technology was situated. The quality went up, and the deliveries improved as a result. It happened again in 2007 when we shifted from sales agencies to wholly owned subsidiaries or distributors, and that required developing offshore teams. It happened in 2009 when I moved the whole product-design team to Portland, Oregon, because that's the place to attract talent to keep our products fresh. These were key pivot points."

Icebreaker is going through another transition. In early 2014 Jeremy transitioned out of the role of CEO and into the dual roles of chairman and creative director. He says, "It was a big decision for me to hand over our business to another CEO, but it's what the company needed. A founder has to be able to see his limitations and bring on the right people."

Icebreaker hired Rob Fyfe, an experienced CEO who is well-versed in operations and growing a consumer company. Prior to joining Icebreaker, Rob was the CEO of Air New Zealand, and was credited with turning around the airline during the economic downturn following the global financial crisis of 2008 and 2009.[36]

These pivots are a hallmark of a Sticky Brand, because when you stop reinventing a business you risk being trapped in the status quo. But change can be scary and it requires constant communication with your team. They need to know where the company is heading and why these changes are important. As Jeremy says, "Internally, whenever I talk about change or strategy it's always authentic. I never lie to my guys. It's never puffery. I never go out punching in the air, and cheering rah rah. I talk them through it, and give them the background, the situation analysis, and our decisions. And I ask them to come on the next phase of the journey."

Keep Pushing

You can achieve remarkable things when your team knows where the company is heading, why the strategy is important, and they have concrete Big Goals to focus their actions. This approach gives your team focus and energy. It propels your company to grow faster than the competition and Punch Outside Its Weight Class. It allows you to reach more customers and fulfill your brand's purpose.

The status quo is the enemy of a Sticky Brand. When things are getting comfortable or success just seems inevitable, it's time to shake things up. What's next? Where does the company need to be in the next three years? How can you reinvent your business to fulfill your brand's purpose?

It's a journey of reinvention, and it never stops.

Exercise: Big Goals and Bold Actions

Objective:

Commit to Big Goals — Big Goals that will energize your brand and drive it to grow through the next revenue plateau.

Gaining Traction

Develop two sets of goals. The first is a big three-year goal. Then break that goal into six smaller goals — goals you will execute every six months to push towards your three-year goal.

Each of the six-month goals functions as a push that will work to overcome the inertia of the current state. A good analogy is to think of this strategy like pushing a car out of a snowdrift. I am an avid snowboarder and live for powder days. But getting to the ski hill in the middle of a snowstorm can have its moments. I have found myself stuck in more than one snowdrift over the years.

Pushing a car out of a snowdrift requires a rocking motion. You get a couple of guys to push, and have another person in the driver's seat. It's a heave-ho process. The driver steps on the gas and everyone pushes, and then they release. The car rocks forward a bit, and then you push again. You do this over and over again until you have enough momentum to break free of the drift.

Apply the same approach to your Big Goals. Start by defining a SMART three-year goal. Where do you want your company and brand to be in three years?

Each of the six-month goals then focuses on specific areas of the business. What processes, systems, talent, or capabilities does your company need to acquire over the next three years to achieve its Big Goal? Look at all aspects of your business to develop the six-month goals: sales, marketing, operations, manufacturing, human resources, finance, partners, distribution, and every other key area of your company.

Ground It in Purpose

Every Big Goal always connects back to your company's purpose. Why does your company exist? What is your brand trying to fulfill?

Define the R — Relevance — in your SMART goal. Why is the Big Goal important for your company and your customers?

Whenever you are developing or reviewing your goals, bring out your company's purpose. You can use Paul Kerr's question, "Guys, are we losing the plot?" Are your goals serving your customers, or not?

Principle 12.5: Choose Your Brand

Sticky Brands are built by people: ambitious, impatient, talented people. People who are not satisfied with the status quo or growing just another business. Sticky Brands are built by people who commit to growing them.

Choose your brand. Grow a brand that stands out in your industry like an orange tree in an evergreen forest.

Build a Sticky Brand

My parents taught me that "it's not the business you've built, but the business you are building."

It was an important lesson. Professionally, 2004 was a very tough year for me. I had quit a lucrative career the year before and I desperately wanted to be even more successful in my parents' company than I had been in my previous position. Instead, I found myself grinding it out with our sales team, dialing for dollars in a business that seemed to be failing. I couldn't believe what I had gotten myself into. On more than one occasion I regretted joining the family business. And at the end of that first year, I was seriously considering going back to the "real world," and proving everyone right about family business failures.

Working in a family business can have a strange dynamic, because consultants and advisers like to say, "Only one in ten family businesses make it to the third generation." It's a depressing stat, and I started to hold onto it when I was struggling in my family's business. I thought I, too, would be just another statistic. But that attitude was wrong.

In this economy and in this market you cannot afford to stand still. It will kill you. Family business or not, companies that succeed through the decades understand that standing still is not an option. This lesson was drilled into me over and over again upon joining my family's business. But change is hard. Doing something differently is often counterintuitive. It's hard to give up infrastructure and processes you have already invested in, and it's hard to stop doing things you are good at. But when the wheels fall off the bus, like they did in my situation, all that resistance goes out the window.

I learned what it meant to be an entrepreneur by going through this challenging period. I was frustrated and scared because I was caught up in the past. I grew up in a family with a successful business, and when I saw the business falling apart around me I didn't know what I was doing wrong. I even thought the failure of the business was my fault. My parents, on the other hand, weren't panicking and thinking the sky was falling. They knew from their own entrepreneurial experiences that you create your own success. What they taught me is that a business has a life cycle, and to be an entrepreneur you have to be prepared to reinvent the business and blaze new trails. What had worked for them in the past was no longer applicable. It was time to change directions.

The moment we committed to changing directions was a breakthrough. We had a mission: grow a Sticky Brand. We were committed to rethinking, reimagining, and rebranding our business. We were committed to growing a business that would make a dent in our industry. And that's what we did.

Jim Gilbert, CEO of Jim Gilbert's Wheels and Deals, likes to say "Every overnight successful business was twenty years in the making." Companies that stand out the most are not built overnight. Behind every Sticky Brand lies a commitment. Jim continues, "We are thirty-four years in the business, but we're fourteen years into the successful part of ours."

Jim is referring to a transition point in the development of the Wheels and Deals brand. Prior to 2000 they were just another independent used car dealership. As discussed in Principle 3: Function That Resonates, it carried an inventory of fifteen to twenty cars, and sold fifteen to twenty cars a month. The catalyst for change was a new entrant into its marketplace. A new dealership opened up that carried one hundred cars on its lot and sold one hundred cars a month. The threat was significant enough to force Wheels and Deals to rethink and reimagine their approach. What kind of business did they really want to build?

Fourteen years later, Jim Gilbert's Wheels and Deals is the largest independent used car dealership in its market. It overcame the competitive threat and beat it, and the company's brand precedes it. Wheels and Deals is known as the "huggable car dealership," and it wraps its customers in service and support they can't find anywhere else.

Growing a Sticky Brand always starts with a choice. What are you going to build? The past is the past, the future is your opportunity. What kind of business and brand are you going to build? The choice is yours.

Built to Last

Sticky Brands are built to last, and so, too, are the companies featured in this book. Half of the businesses we have discussed are multi-generational family businesses — privately held companies that are owned and operated by families. These companies have stood the test of time, and many have been operating for twenty, fifty, or even one hundred years. For example, Purdys Chocolatier was founded in 1907, Pizza Nova was founded in 1963, and Cardinal Couriers was founded in 1978. These companies have grown through the generations because they adapt and evolve. They have taken a long view of their brand and made the investments necessary to grow a brand that lasts.

Steve Jobs said, "I hate it when people call themselves 'entrepreneurs' when what they're really trying to do is launch a startup and then sell or go public, so they can cash in and move on. They're unwilling to do the work it takes to build a real company, which is the hardest work in business. That's how you really make a contribution and add to the legacy of those who went before. You build a company that will still stand for something a generation or two from now."

The companies featured in this book echo those sentiments:

- Bob Spiers, CEO of ProVision IT, said, "Before we even launched, I had a goal to build a 'self-sustaining enterprise.' That was the phrase that really resonated with me. And what that meant was to have the structure, a lasting value, and the processes, culture, and understanding of how to operate the right way so the business would self-propel — so it would be self-sustaining."
- David Cronin, CTO of DevFacto, said, "If we were building this company for sale we would have done things differently.… We're building our company so that our employees can buy it from us in the future. That's our plan. We are building a culture that people love so much they are willing to put their own money into it."
- Shaun Muldoon, CEO of Muldoon's Coffee, said, "As we grow the business, I don't want to be twice as big, but half as good. That would just be such a disappointment for everyone involved."

These business owners are committed to the long haul. They are building organizations that serve their customers and create a legacy. This commitment to the long view creates a competitive advantage, because you cannot make investments in your company, people, or brand if you are only considering the next ninety days.

Think of the generation that comes after you. Build a company and a brand that has a strong foundation. One that isn't dependent on you or your management team. Build a foundation that has longevity and can be transitioned onto the next generation, who will take the brand even farther.

Some Assembly Required

There are a lot of moving parts to growing a Sticky Brand. It takes more than a great product and an innovative marketing strategy. It requires putting all the pieces together.

The Principles, stories, and exercises discussed in this book demonstrate the range and depth that goes into growing a Sticky Brand. The companies featured in these pages have all made deliberate choices to challenge the giants of their industry, to innovate, and to find better ways to serve their customers. They are Positioned to Win, because they choose where to play and how to win. They have Authentic Differentiation and work to make their brands visibly different. They Punch Outside Their Weight Class, because they blow their horns and attract customers to them. They Over Commit and Over Deliver by investing in their people and cultures, and energize them with Big Goals.

The process of growing a Sticky Brand can seem overwhelming when you look at all the parts, but don't let that deter you. The 12.5 Principles provide a structure so you can implement the ideas in your business. Focus on your needs and goals for the next six to twelve months. Where is your business heading? What challenges or obstacles must you overcome? What are your Big Goals? What do you need to accomplish to reach them?

Your priorities and needs will shift on a quarterly basis. Use this book as a playbook and a reference guide. Part 1 provides the insight and structure on positioning and defining how your business will win. Part 2 focuses on the principles of differentiating your brand and making it stand out like an orange tree in an evergreen forest. Part 3 provides the tools to grow brand awareness and driving sales. Part 4 will help you grow a culture that is results-oriented and focused on creating an incredible brand.

Keep this book handy. It's your branding playbook to seek inspiration and ideas.

Make a Commitment

Growing a Sticky Brand has a lot of benefits: increased sales, adoring customers, engaged employees, competitive immunity, and higher profits. But getting there, getting to the point where your brand stands out like an orange tree in an evergreen forest, is a commitment. Companies don't just proclaim, "Our brand is sticky." No. They commit to building a Sticky Brand, and that can take years or even decades of innovation, experimentation, and hard work.

Are you prepared to make that commitment?

I'm not asking if your company is prepared for that journey. I'm asking *you*, because this commitment is personal. It starts with you deciding, "This is what *I* want. This is what *I* am pursuing. This is *my* goal." Growing a Sticky Brand is a personal commitment. It isn't a job or a stepping stone in your career. Growing a Sticky Brand is a way of life.

If you are prepared for the journey, and you are excited about the prospect of growing your company's brand, you have an amazing road ahead of you. Sticky Brands leave an indelible mark on lives they touch: employees, customers, partners, and the communities around them. They make an impact that an average brand could only dream of.

The choice rests with you.

Growing a Sticky Brand is a choice. It's a choice to stand out and be remarkable. It's a choice to build meaningful relationships with your customers. It's a choice to cut your own path and innovate in your industry. Growing a Sticky Brand is your choice to stand out, attract customers, and drive sales.

Make the choice, and implement each of the Principles discussed in the book to make your company a Sticky Brand.

Featured Brands

Note:  denotes a family-owned business.

Arment Dietrich

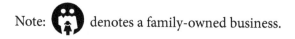

Arment Dietrich is a Chicago-based integrated marketing communications firm. It has experts across North America who specialize in the four media types: paid, earned, shared, and owned.

www.armentdietrich.com

Pages 123–27

Beau's All Natural Brewing Co.

Beau's All Natural Brewing Co. is a family-run craft brewery founded in 2006. Beau's brews interesting, tasty beers using the highest-quality organic ingredients and local spring water.

www.beaus.ca

Pages 69–74

Brilliant™

Brilliant™ is a staffing, search, and management resources firm with offices in Chicago and southern Florida. It provides solutions to companies with hiring needs and candidates looking to enhance their careers.

www.brilliantfs.com

Pages 129–32

Cardinal Couriers

Cardinal Couriers is a mid-sized, high-performing delivery service company. It provides pre-8:00 a.m. delivery services for time-sensitive goods for companies in Ontario and Quebec, Canada.

www.cardinalcouriers.com

Pages 34–36

The Central Group

The Central Group is a retail marketing display and packaging company. It focuses on driving "performance-at-retail" through its retailer expertise, design innovation, unique shopper research, manufacturing, and enterprise systems.

www.centralgrp.com

Pages 57–62

DECO Windshield Repair

DECO Windshield Repair fixes windshield chips. It specializes in auto-glass repair, and provides fast, professional service to fix a chip or small crack while you wait or run errands.

www.decorepair.com

Pages 89–92

Deighton Associates Limited

Deighton Associates develops dTIMS, the leading infrastructure asset management software system. Deighton's solutions are used globally by departments of transportation and large industrial firms.

www.deighton.com

Pages 33–34

DevFacto Technologies

DevFacto is a Microsoft Gold Certified consulting company that delivers end-to-end software solutions. It specializes in portals and collaboration, custom software, mobility, and managed services.

www.devfacto.com

Pages 156–58

FeedBlitz

feedblitz

FeedBlitz helps bloggers and businesses get their words out to their audience. The company sends, brands, and tracks email, RSS feeds, tweets, Facebook updates, and more, while minimizing the extra work for the publisher.

www.feedblitz.com

Pages 171–72

Icebreaker Inc.

Icebreaker designs and manufactures merino clothing for the outdoors, technical sports, and lifestyle. Icebreaker is based in Auckland, New Zealand, and is sold in more than four thousand stores in forty-four countries.

www.icebreaker.com

Pages 185–87

Jim Gilbert's Wheels and Deals

Jim Gilbert's Wheels and Deals is "Canada's Huggable Car Dealer," selling "slightly used cars." It is the most referred used car dealer in New Brunswick, and is one of the largest in Eastern Canada.

www.wheelsanddeals.ca

Pages 53–57

🐸 LEAPJob

LEAPJob is a sales and marketing recruiting firm based in Toronto, Canada. It applies focused methodology, research, and expertise to find the sales and marketing talent its clients want and need.

www.leapjob.com

Pages 73–77

🐸 Macpek

Macpek is a second-generation family-operated business that specializes in the distribution of truck parts and aluminum and steel wheels for cars.

www.macpek.com

Pages 158–60

🐸 Muldoon's Coffee

Muldoon's Coffee, the evolution of the corporate coffee service in Toronto, delivering fresh-roasted coffee in every brewing method, from whole bean to the unique "green" single-serve system.

www.muldoonscoffee.com

Pages 96–99

National Logistics Services

National Logistics Services is the logistics supplier for the fashion and footwear industry. It understands the intricacies of the Canadian retail landscape, both for business-to-business and e-commerce logistics.

www.nls.ca

Pages 42–44

Neatfreak Group Inc.

neatfreak!
THE HOME ORGANIZATION COMPANY™

Neatfreak designs, manufactures, and distributes innovative home-organization products to retailers around the world. It provides imaginative solutions that keeps things organized and helps to control chaos in the home.

www.neatfreak.com

Pages 144–45

Pizza Nova

Pizza Nova is a leading pizza chain in Ontario, Canada with over 130 locations. Pizza Nova pride itself on the simple fact that it delivers quality and its customers "Taste the Difference."

www.pizzanova.com

Pages 166–68

ProVision IT Resources

ProVision is a Toronto-based company offering contract and recruitment services, with clients primarily in Ontario, Canada. It has been operating since 2002.

www.provisionit.ca

Pages 40–42

Purdys Chocolatier

Purdys Chocolatier is Canada's largest retailer of specialty chocolate. Family owned and operated since 1907, Purdys' chocolates are made in its Vancouver factory kitchen using only the finest ingredients from around the world.

www.purdys.com

Pages 84–89

Quarry Integrated Communications

Quarry is an integrated marketing communications firm headquartered in St. Jacobs, Canada. Its expertise is in being "the buyer experience agency for savvy marketers who want to transform their business brands."

www.quarry.com

Pages 36–37

Quartet Service Inc.

Quartet provides outsourced IT services such as helpdesk, on-site service, designing, and building IT networks, as well as a variety of cloud-based services. Its packages are customized to meet the requirements of mid-market companies.

www.quartetservice.com

Pages 17–18

Scalar Decisions

Scalar Decisions is an IT solution provider. It architects, implements, and manages mission-critical IT systems across Canada. It is also one of Canada's fastest-growing companies.

www.scalar.ca

Pages 183–85

Silverline

Silverline is a Salesforce Gold Cloud Alliance Partner headquartered in New York City. It focuses exclusively on the end-to-end implementation of *Salesforce.com* products and powerful third party apps.

www.silverlinecrm.com

Pages 178–80

Versature

Business phone service. Evolved.

Versature is a business phone service, delivering Hosted PBX and VoIP phone services to small- and mid-sized companies across Canada. Its advanced features and responsive customer service improve productivity and reduce costs.

www.versature.com

Pages 110–12

WildPlay Element Parks

WildPlay provides unique aerial adventures, from bungee jumps to zip lines. Its "elements" of primal fun and games encourage humans of diverse abilities to play hard and fear less in nature-based recreation.

www.wildplay.com

Pages 152–55

Acknowledgements

Writing may seem like a solitary endeavor, but it takes a lot of people to put a book together. This was a team effort and I am truly grateful to everyone who supported me, encouraged me, and helped me along the way. Thank you!

My parents: Donna and Marcus gave me the opportunity to be an entrepreneur. I gained a lifetime of experiences and knowledge working beside them. They taught me what it means to chase my dreams, and how to continually innovate and drive for something greater than myself. They are my biggest supporters. They have read every word I've ever written — sometimes more than once.

My validation team: Dr. Mary Donohue, Paul Brent, Don Loney, Christie Lamenzo, Stephen Miller, Jim Stewart, and Cathleen Colehour. This book has their fingerprints all over it.

My teammates at Dundurn: Publisher Kirk Howard bet on me, and he, Margaret Bryant, Laura Boyle, Karen McMullin, and the rest of the Dundurn team supported me and helped to create this book. Michael Melgaard's insightful editing and suggestions stretched my thinking and made this book what it is. I didn't like writing each chapter two or three times, but I am so glad I did.

My teammates at Design & Develop: Paul Sveda designed the book cover and graphics, and Opal Gamble always brought a dose of reality and logic. They helped me put my best foot forward.

The connectors: To research this book I profiled over 150 companies in twelve months. I connected with fascinating companies from around the world thanks to several referral partners: Lorraine Bauer, Paul

MacDonald, Sheila Simms, and Emma Ramos at the Canadian Association of Family Enterprise (CAFE); Tammy Schuiling, Ken MacLeod, and Catherine Osler at TEC Canada; Gini Dietrich and Laura Petrolino at Arment Dietrich; Kelly Willis; Adrian Woodlife; Adam Green; Jordan Gould; and the members of the Sticky Branding LinkedIn group.

The community: The Sticky Branding community is an endless source of ideas, inspiration, and friendships. The people, discussions, and sharing always inspire me and feed my curiosity.

Notes

1. "Statistics about Business Size (including Small Business) from the U.S. Census Bureau," United States Census Bureau, *www.census. gov/econ/smallbus.html*.
2. Erik Sherman, "Apple's Ad Budget Hits $1 Billion," CBS News, January 7, 2013, *www.cbsnews.com/news/apples-ad-budget-hits-1-billion*.
3. Richard Florida, *The Great Reset: How New Ways Of Living and Working Drive Post-Crash Prosperity* (Toronto: Random House Canada, 2010), 157.
4. A.G. Lafley and Roger L. Martin, *Playing to Win: How Strategy Really Works* (Boston: Harvard Business Review Press), 20.
5. Richard M. Perloff. *The Dynamics of Persuasion: Communication and Attitudes in the 21st Century* (New York: Lawrence Erlbaum Associates, 2008), 181–82.
6. Adam Morgan, *Eating the Big Fish: How Challenger Brands Can Compete Against Brand Leaders, Second Edition* (New York: John Wiley & Sons, Inc., 2009), 4.
7. "Dylex Agrees to Sell Major Assets to U.S. Company," *Ottawa Business Journal*, August 24, *2000, www.obj.ca/Other/Archives/2000-08-24/article-2238592/Dylex-agrees-to-sell-major-assets-to-U.S.-company/1*.
8. "Best Global Brands 2013," *Interbrand*, September 30, 2013, *www. interbrand.com/en/best-global-brands/2013/Best-Global-Brands-2013-Brand-View.aspx*.
9. "Top 100 Brand Ranking," *BrandZ*, May 20, 2013, *www.millward-

brown.com/brandz/2013/Top100/Docs/2013_BrandZ_Top100_Chart.
pdf.

10. David A. Aaker, *Managing Brand Equity: Capitalizing on the Value of a Brand Name* (New York: Free Press, 1991), 13–16.

11. Perloff, *The Dynamics of Persuasion*, 236.

12. Kelton V.L. Rhoads and Robert B. Cialdini, "The Business of Influence: Principles That Lead to Success in Commercial Settings," *The Persuasion Handbook: Development in Theory and Practice* (California: Sage Publications, 2002), 532–33.

13. E.J. Schultz, "Anheuser-Busch President Dave Peacock Steps Down," *Advertising Age*, January 23, 2012, *adage.com/article/news/ab-president-dave-peacock-steps/232291/*.

14. "Craft Brewing Statistics: Facts," Brewers Association, January 5, 2014, *www.brewersassociation.org/pages/business-tools/craft-brewing-statistics/facts*.

15. Gerald Zaltman and Lindsay H. Zaltman, *Marketing Metaphoria: What Deep Metaphors Reveal about the Minds of Consumers* (Boston: Harvard Business Press, 2008), xv.

16. Gerald Zaltman, *How Customers Think: Essential Insights Into the Mind of the Market* (Boston: Harvard Business Press, 2002), 214.

17. Stephanie Milot, "Apple Stores Set New Revenue-Per-Visitor Record," *PCMag.com*, May 20, 2013, *www.pcmag.com/article2/0,2817,2419228,00.asp*.

18. Stephanie Milot, "Apple Stores Top Tiffany's in Retail Sales per Square Foot," *PCMag.com*, November 13, 2012, *www.pcmag.com/article2/0,2817,2412094,00.asp*.

19. "#86, DECO Windshield Repair Inc." Profit 500 2013 Ranking, *Profit Magazine, www.profitguide.com/microsite/profit500/2013/ranking/86-deco-windshield-repair-inc*.

20. "Dove Real Beauty Sketches," *realbeautysketches.dove.ca*.

21. Lois Kelly, *Beyond Buzz: The Next Generation of Word-of-Mouth Marketing* (New York: AMACOM, 2007), 61–62.

22. "Dove's Sketches of Real Women Hit 30 Million Views, Tops Viral Chart," *AdAge*, April 24, 2013, *adage.com/article/the-viral-video-chart/dove-s-sketches-real-women-top-viral-chart/241055*.

23. "About LinkedIn," LinkedIn, *press.linkedin.com/about.*

24. Michael Hyatt, *Platform: Get Noticed in a Noisy World* (Nashville: Thomas Nelson, 2012), xviii.

25. Clay Shirky, *Cognitive Surplus: Creativity and Generosity in a Connected Age* (New York: Penguin Press, 2010), 198–201.

26. Seth Godin, "Advice For Authors," August 2, 2006, *sethgodin.typepad.com/seths_blog/2006/08/advice_for_auth.html.*

27. Charles Arthur, "How the 'Value Trap' Squeezes Windows PC makers' revenues and profits," Guardian News and Media Limited, January 9, 2014, *www.theguardian.com/technology/2014/jan/09/pc-value-trap-windows-chrome-hp-dell-lenovo-asus-acer.*

28. Jim Collins, *Good to Great: Why Some Companies Make the Leap … And Others Don't* (New York: HarperCollins Publishers Inc., 2001), 54.

29. "ENRON Annual Report 1998," p. 71, *picker.uchicago.edu/Enron/EnronAnnualReport1998.pdf.*

30. "Top 10 Canadian Mobile Technology Companies," 2014 Branham300 List, Branham Group Inc., *www.branham300.com/index.php?year=2014&listing=17.*

31. Walter Isaacson, *Steve Jobs* (New York: Simon & Schuster, 2011), 47–48.

32. Susan Casey, "Blueprint for Green Business," *Fortune*, May 29, 2007.

33. K. Anders Ericsson, Michael J. Prietula, and Edward T. Cokely, "The Making of an Expert," *Harvard Business Review*, July 2007.

34. David A. Aaker, *Brand Relevance: Making Competitors Irrelevant* (San Francisco: Jossey-Bass, 2011), 312.

35. A.G. Lafley and Roger L. Martin, *Playing to Win: How Strategy Really Works* (Boston: Harvard Business Review Press), 36.

36. "Icebreaker Appoints Rob Fyfe as Chief Executive Officer," Icebreaker, May 26, 2014, *media.icebreaker.com/index.php?s=43&item=361.*

Index

About the Author

Jeremy Miller is a Brand Builder, Speaker, and the President of Sticky Branding — a brand building agency.

After rebranding his family's business, Jeremy embarked on a decade long study of how small- and mid-sized companies create incredible brands. Since 2005 he has interviewed thousands of CEOs and business owners and profiled hundreds of companies across dozens of sectors.

Jeremy works with companies to make them stand out, challenge the giants of their industry, and grow incredible brands. He is a sought after speaker delivering highly entertaining and informative keynotes speeches on branding and business development. He knows what it takes to grow a Sticky Brand and how you can do it too.

For more information visit *www.stickybranding.com.*

Also Available from Dundurn

TOUCH
by Tod Maffin and Mark Blevis

For better or worse, digital business has fundamentally changed how organizations hire staff, market their services, and connect with stakeholders. The problem is, in an effort to use technology to connect with people more effectively, we have lost the humanity — that critical person-to-person connection — that is the engine of commerce:

- Hiring is done by automated keyword searches.
- Offices have regressed to sterile, highly controlled environments.
- Staff rely exclusively on template responses.
- Websites are designed for search engines, not people.
- Leaders are focusing on arbitrary and antiquated "best practices."

In a world filled with complicated web forms and digital marketing services, we have lost the "human" element in how we run our organizations. TOUCH identifies these problems in stark terms, then provide business leaders in all types of organizations — private to public sector, small to enterprise business — with real-world, tested solutions.

Available at your favourite bookseller

DUNDURN

Visit us at
Dundurn.com
@dundurnpress
Facebook.com/dundurnpress
Pinterest.com/dundurnpress